THE POET AS EXPERIENCER

Before you start to read this book, take this moment to think about making a donation to punctum books, an independent non-profit press,

@ https://punctumbooks.com/support/

If you're reading the e-book, you can click on the image below to go directly to our donations site. Any amount, no matter the size, is appreciated and will help us to keep our ship of fools afloat. Contributions from dedicated readers will also help us to keep our commons open and to cultivate new work that can't find a welcoming port elsewhere. Our adventure is not possible without your support.

Vive la Open Access.

Fig. 1. Detail from Hieronymus Bosch, *Ship of Fools* (1490–1500)

THE POET AS EXPERIENCER: WALLACE STEVENS AND NONHUMAN INTELLIGENCE.
Copyright © 2025 by Adam Staley Groves. This work carries a Creative Commons BY-NC-SA 4.0 International license, which means that you are free to copy and redistribute the material in any medium or format, and you may also remix, transform, and build upon the material, as long as you clearly attribute the work to the author (but not in a way that suggests the author or punctum books endorses you and your work), you do not use this work for commercial gain in any form whatsoever, and that for any remixing and transformation, you distribute your rebuild under the same license. http://creativecommons.org/licenses/by-nc-sa/4.0/

Published in 2025 by punctum books, Earth, Milky Way.
https://punctumbooks.com

ISBN-13: 978-1-68571-276-1 (print)
ISBN-13: 978-1-68571-277-8 (ePDF)

DOI: 10.53288/0296.1.00

LCCN: 2025940850
Library of Congress Cataloging Data is available from the Library of Congress

Editing: Vincent W.J. van Gerven Oei and SAJ
Book design: Hatim Eujayl
Cover image: Adam Staley Groves
Cover design: Vincent W.J. van Gerven Oei

spontaneous acts of scholarly combustion

HIC SVNT MONSTRA

The Poet As Experiencer

*Wallace Stevens and
Nonhuman Intelligence*

Adam Staley Groves

Contents

Preface · 13

1. Five Poems of High Strangeness · 23
2. Credible Rhetoric · 45
3. Owl's Palace · 63
4. The Blue Gods of Organismus · 81
5. Xretism · 109
6. The Emergence of Abstraction · 119
7. The Affirmation of John Mack · 137
8. Poetry Itself · 149

Bibliography · 177

Acknowledgments

To be honest one must acknowledge themselves, each and every day, for doing this human thing. Thank you for not giving in, giving up, or letting the possibility for truth or the nature of reality evade.

Specific to the question of the imagination, I would like to sincerely acknowledge my teacher Wolfgang Schirmacher. Furthermore, I thank Wolfgang's European Graduate School (EGS), from which this study was seeded. It was Wolfgang who posed this question in a seminar many years ago in Saas-Fee and equally demonstrated a commitment to the embodiment of knowledge, if not the hazards of it.

As for poetry, in the early years of graduate study, I wish to acknowledge the late Pierre Alferi, who exemplified the very energy of poetry and its intelligence at such a crucial and transformative time in my life. And of course, Laurence Rickels, Avital Ronell, and Hubertus von Amelunxen, who supported and inspired me.

I wish to acknowledge, with all sincerity and joy, the most formidable Judith Balso whose understanding of Wallace Stevens and Fernando Pessoa were decisive and transformative. Her conceptualizations presented an unrivaled genius, one which decisively shifted my interest to the theory of poetry. Equally owe thanks to Philippe Beck whose guidance, confidence, example, intelligence, and humor supplied affirmation in the most challenging, late hours of research on Wallace Stevens, specifically regarding poetry, its theory, and philosophy.

Thank you to Christopher Fynsk and in particular the University of Aberdeen, which gave a home to my doctoral studies on Stevens, Jean Wahl, and the theory of poetry. I wish to thank Torgeir Fjeld for giving my research a space to develop and grow when everything else seemed at an end.

To the UFO researchers, experiencers, and thinkers out there, to those who take genuine risks both intellectually, spiritually, and emotionally to learn if not earn a deeper understanding of the nature of reality: Thank you.

And most certainly, I owe my deep gratitude to Dan Hughes, Natalie Smolenski, John Van Houdt, and the editor and publisher of this book, Vincent W.J. van Gerven Oei, who has been with me one hundred percent of the way. These four bore witness to the very beginning of this book. To those many friends old and new that will not be named but know who they are; to those who put up with me, seriously; and indeed, to those who would otherwise be enemies: do not flatter yourself, you are loved. Finally, to the many students I have had the pleasure to think with over the years: thank you with all sincerity.

Preface

> The nature of reality is fundamentally not government information.
> —Col. Karl Knell[1]

> Alas, our technology has marched ahead of our spiritual and social evolution, making us, frankly, a dangerous people.
> —Steven M. Greer[2]

The UFO phenomenon is a complex, fast-changing, and beguiling subject. It is ever prone to disinformation, stigma, and various pejoratives. For most of its modern history academics have avoided the subject. Yet in 2017 when *The New York Times* published its story "Glowing Auras and 'Black Money': The Pentagon's Mysterious U.F.O. Program," something changed. UFOs were real, at least, for those who read the *Times*.[3] In parallel, a group called "To The Stars Academy" emerged, featuring one

---

1 SALT, "'Zero Doubt' Non-Human Intelligence on Earth — Col. Karl Nell & Alex Klokus | SALT iConnections NY," *YouTube*, May 22, 2024, https://www.youtube.com/watch?v=RploFrdJWfs.
2 Steven M. Greer, *Hidden Truth: Forbidden Knowledge* (ZTT Consulting, 2013), 37.
3 Helene Cooper, Ralph Blumenthal, and Leslie Kean, "Glowing Auras and 'Black Money': The Pentagon's Mysterious U.F.O. Program," *The New York*

punk rock celebrity and luminous UFO researchers with ties to Scientology, US defense, and counterintelligence.[4] Something was afoot, yet at the time I did not indulge. I was gainfully employed as a university lecturer and focused on my career. Long into my own denial, I was not about to risk a lifetime of work by touching Midas. What caught my attention, however, was the 2023 congressional testimony made by whistleblower and former Air Force counterintelligence officer David Grusch.[5] It was obvious that the American public was being prepared for UFO disclosure. If the phenomenon was officially real, the UFO was a fringe topic no longer — permission granted.

There are varying opinions on Grusch, but despite these the effect his testimony had was triggering. Truth be told, the pandemic changed me in ways I am still dealing with. Right as it began, I found myself once more an adjunct, questioning whether I should, once and for all, end my career. As an independent researcher, I have, like many others, endured the erosion if not banalization of the humanities in the last two decades. And up to 2023 I was still careful of what I would indulge in, replaying the normative suppression one must in order to survive and feed their family. Yet I was hardly surviving. I already made things difficult having spent years studying the links between modern poetry, its theory, and "continental philosophy." Applying it where I could to topics of public concern was good alchemy, a feat in itself, despite how necessary I knew it to be.

If Grusch triggered me, it had little to do with what he said, but rather with how I understood the phenomenon decades before. Born at the end of Generation X, I came of age through the 1980s and '90s. Many late nights and early mornings were

---

Times, December 16, 2017, https://www.nytimes.com/2017/12/16/us/politics/pentagon-program-ufo-harry-reid.html.

4 *To The Stars: Bringing You the Future,* https://tothestars.media/pages/about.

5 7NEWS Australia, "David Grusch UFO/UAP bombshells: Ross Coulthart reveals the inside story," *YouTube,* July 27, 2023, https://www.youtube.com/watch?v=x_9gTDXF9Vc.

spent listening to Art Bell while working third-shift jobs trying to survive high school. Some of my friends and I were mystically inclined, though uneducated and poor. We were atypically midwestern, dabbling in astrology, chiromancy, and other such subjects. A few of my high school teachers encouraged us to meditate, to open our minds and intellects to the cosmos and explore poetry and philosophy. Indeed, I went to a nontraditional school, yet the skeptic in me was always operative. There is a material world, after all, and one must survive. Yet a little hippie thinking never hurts.

The core of my skepticism was not a lack of belief in the phenomenon, not even the opposite. In fact, it had nothing to do with my own belief, but rather a suspicion of others' beliefs. How do *you* know? Too much Art Bell made me paranoid, even if I liked John Lear and Major Ed Dames. The truth is that people who believed in aliens at that time often smoked a lot of weed, adorning their dirty bongs with the prerequisite stickers, or indulging in all-night raves and finding their soul through LSD and nitrous. None of that was for me. And as Y2K came and went, I felt more and more the fool for having entertained notions beyond those that I knew were true, those of my own experiences.

The metaphysical 1990s soon became the terroristic 2000s, and I finally, barely, got into state university. At first, all I could think about was getting a job. I did not want to be poor anymore, but I also didn't care to be rich. I just wanted a decent, normal life and do something good for society. Previously I lived the life of a naïve musician and artist, traversing the fringe cultures of the DIY world and subculture politics. I got out when a then nascent force of social media was quickly replacing the world of tapes and records with CDs and electronically procured fan bases. In university I was fully immersed in the fantasy world of American collegiate life. I was a bit older than the other freshmen, so I made friends with graduate students who studied chemistry. To my oft aggressively progressive professors, I featured all the wrong signifiers and felt more like a burden. I grew bored with journalism and faculty politics, so took a second, liberal arts major. That changed nothing.

Universities are best at destroying and rebuilding minds. So naturally I began to unravel but decided to do the rebuilding myself. One evening I was reviewing a paper for my history class and noticed syllabic and thematic patterns. Interest was once more piqued in what I later understood to be "poetry itself." So, I returned to poetry, began writing it again and sought to introduce myself to campus professors and poets, to literature. No one was interested. It was around then that I started studying philosophy once more and this time I had used book stores to supply me. Needless to say, this did not help much in terms of careering and I fell further into my own world. That is, until I was accepted to graduate school in Switzerland to study philosophy.

Graduate school will destroy and rebuild you too. You might even enjoy it, as did I. While there is much to say about it, I need to get to the point. Philosophy I love, no doubt, but it was poetry and, in particular, a few poets, who found me. This can be difficult for some to accept but it hardly matters. Poetry chooses you; you do not choose it. But in the end we are not talking about poems or poets, but rather poetry itself. So please, do not waste time on clichés: "a poet who didn't know it" is not what I mean. I knew it, just not by that name. Today, when people talk about the phenomenon all over the internet and through podcasts, I reach back two decades and recall what it was like to experience synchronicity without constantly ingesting the revelations of others, to experience that, no matter where I went in the world, things were consistently beyond coincidence. However, I was in graduate school and by that point desirous of becoming a university professor, a teacher more than anything else who now needed to work to pay off their debt. Quickly and in the harshest ways I learnt the reality of the industry. As I embarked on my career, I discovered institutions oft care not for good change, open discourse, or progress. That faculties are built by insider connections and retaining power. Those who are elevated within support the hubris of their superior above. That elation inside of you — keep it down. Your openness to spirituality — keep it quiet. Your questioning of naturalism and materialism — shhhh.

It comes to this. There were three times I was returned to the same place from which an understanding of my existence took form. A place in memory I habitually repressed. By returned I mean broken down through my later educational life experiences. Each time that I reified the truth of my strange experiences I learned to say less and less about it; drawing confidence but not indulging my distrust in others' beliefs. The place, that is, my first experience, was in August of 1979, when, barely three years old, I recalled a past life to my mother and aunt while visiting the grave of my father's mother. They were understandably shocked that I knew precise details of my grandmother, the nature of her death in late 1975, how she felt about her name, what it looked like soon after she passed, what she died of, her double mastectomy, and so forth. They both wrote it down and luckily saved these documents, as I would go so far in my own disbelief that I needed them to prove to myself what I already knew. This past life I continued to remark on as a young child as well as chirping out messages about visiting divinities, once remarking that "Jesus is coming back, but he's not what you think he is." This and other experiences characterized my earliest years. While I retained some memories, I often felt oppressed by the whole thing.

By the age of nine, I had my first visual experience with what I now understand to be a nonhuman intelligence. It was not a ghost; it was very much there. It was not a spirit, as I know them to be now. It happened as I woke from an afternoon nap. Then I observed a very tall male figure outside my window. He was dressed in travelers clothing of another time, wearing a hat, and a rucksack. He was watching me. I must not have felt that threatened, as I recall rolling over and trying to fall back asleep. I soon forgot about it and did not recall this for many years. The uncanny quality of this experience is as clear today as it was then. By the age of twelve I had an involuntary out-of-body experience. I found myself instantaneously in the ceiling, looking down at my body sitting in a chair. As I fell fast back into my body, there was a faint but discernable ball passing through the living room, left to right. There was a message, but I could not understand it beyond sensing the true goodness of a familiar, if not profound love.

As a teenager I avoided drugs and alcohol. Drinking was not a thing until the age of twenty-six. I doubt I would have developed my meditation as I had in those years if I did. The meditation practiced, particular to my late teens and early twenties, led to other insights and confidences oft kept to myself. There was a series of precognitive dreams, for example, but these were often of mundane tasks in places I had not yet been, only to find myself doing the same thing later. Occasionally I would tell people but learned fast through playful ridicule not to speak about it. There were other experiences, some were dark in nature, and these I am still trying to understand. And then there was the death of a very dear and close friend, whom I remained in contact with for many years after. Both in dreams and while awake.

I know how this sounds, but I no longer worry about that. The point is to reveal my personal interest in the phenomenon, particular to poetry. For most of us do not receive poetry beyond trite lyrics and that stodgy academic criticism few bother to read. This has fed our ignorance of what is a most vital mind. Thus, what I mean by poetry itself concerns an elemental if not productive aspect of the phenomenon, that is, our role in its manifestation and testimony. Without doubt it concerns the imagination which has been the primary focus of my research for many years.

The fact is that by 2022 I had sworn off studies of Wallace Stevens, philosophy, and intellectual matters all together. I quit my paltry adjunct job which made me feel worse by the day. I stopped reading or caring about the whole thing. Yes, I had spent most of my life studying and learning, benefiting from my education. However, this world seemed headed in the opposite direction more than ever before. For a few years I had been headed to this point, run out of full-time university work prior to the pandemic, then going through lockdowns. I experienced ego death in a most slow-grinding way, yet there was art, music, and genuine friendship which appeared simultaneously — which kept me going. If everything I did outside of that became parodic and absurd, I soon realized a fourth educational destruction had taken place, albeit in the school of my own hubris. This time, as I returned to the place of my first experiences, I did not stuff it down. I let it slowly come to the surface and began the completion of my own ontological shock.

David Grusch's testimony triggered a notion that fed an inability to not check it out further. I started reading again and soon encountered UFO lore, something I never bothered to read. I went through as much as I could. Truth be told, I have been down rabbit holes before. But this was not a rabbit hole. All of this seemed quite familiar, having the sturdy ground of philosophy to gird my brain. It was only when I read Whitley Strieber and John Mack, as well as Richard Dolan, that I was compelled to return to Wallace Stevens, in particular his poem "Owl's Clover." What I found was an entirely new poet, *a poet as experiencer.* The odd thing is that my previous study of Stevens was directed at his theoretical prose as existing criticism tends to ignore it. As today, in those years I was convinced it was special, remarkable enough to write a second doctoral dissertation nearly a decade ago. The poetry was a secondary matter, a strategic move I suppose, as the prose theory was more or less unheralded. Why I didn't incorporate a study of the poetry still evades me — that is, I wasn't ready, it had not reached out to me or, quite simply, it wasn't time.

I should clarify that this is not about me although without my own self-disclosure none of this would have made sense. Stevens was *an experiencer,* that much is clear; despite lacking terminology for it, he became a believer in the phenomenon early on in life. From this we have much more to learn than what I could summon here, but I believe, sincerely, his is an important contribution to the history and future of disclosure. Some of the writing takes a skeptical tone for the sake of objectivity and fair play. As for poetry, as a subject of academic study, it is incongruent with the status quo of "Wallace Stevens criticism," a realm which has had many battles with philosophy and theory in the past. Of that, I could only wish for a bit of backlash.

In terms of philosophy, what I have to say will likely trouble a few. Despite the fact that philosophy has made a resurgence, in particular a return to panpsychism, the authoritarian figure of this or that science popularizer still casts shame upon us. Conversely it is often the case, no more clearly than in the exchanges between Martin Heidegger, Jacques Derrida, and Paul Celan, that philosophy reliably appropriates thus sophisticates what the poet reveals. In other words, it will please nobody who believes philosophy is the ultimate form of the formless — that it is not. Finally, by divulging my own experiences, I hope to have cleared in advance any questions of my own credibility. I have what I need. For me the phenomenon is not a matter of belief. It is a matter of fact.

Since Grusch's testimony, and certainly before it, ufology has flourished in the podcast world. More recently it has made inroads into the mainstream academy. Jeffrey J. Kripal, Diana Walsh Pasulka, Michael P. Masters, Danny Sheehan, Jacques Vallée, Steven M. Greer, Avi Loeb, Ross Coulthart, Garry P. Nolan, Sean Esbjörn-Hargens, and Jeffrey Mishlove are just some of the names in rotation worth investigating. In terms of the phenomenon, this book is not meant to teach the uninitiated; that work I assume to be the reader's job. With that said, engaging the phenomenon is no easy task, so I have made efforts to inform as there are plenty of lies and deceptions afoot and most certainly one will get mud on their boots.

Within this book the timeline of Wallace Stevens's life is woven. I tried to keep new readers in mind, but it is not biographical. However, there are many references to poems and events which would be best supported by the following books: The Library of America's *Wallace Stevens Collected Poetry and Prose* and Peter Brazaeu's *Parts of a World: Wallace Stevens Remembered*. Regarding the UFO phenomenon, those new to this subject seeking a sturdy reference should acquire a copy of Richard Dolan's *UFOs for the 21st Century Mind*.[6]

...

This book is organized in the following way.

In Chapter One, five poems are examined which suggest Wallace Stevens experienced missing time during the first decades of the twentieth century. Speculation over alien abduction is considered as well as other degrees of contact with nonhuman intelligences (NHIs). This is followed by a consideration of Jungian projection, that of the mandala, in order to situate Stevens within the variegated discussion of the phenomenon in general. Surmised is contact with NHIs and eventually, through psychical change, a willful commensuration with these intelligences.

Chapter Two examines Stevens's rhetoric and disposition. Questions about Stevens's cognizance of NHI in this early period are also considered. A timeline is further established as to the motive and development of the poet's theory resultant of a growing cognizance of NHI.

Chapters Three and Four examine the journals of 1900–1904 in detail. Here I seek to ground the testimony of his poetry with prosaic accounts of probable NHI experiences and missing time. Throughout, key moments of verse are read in parallel with studied aspects by ufologists and researchers of the phenomenon. These chapters integrate findings of the prior chapters and reference Stevens's theory of poetry.

Chapter Five is a brief comparison with Albert Coe, a relatively unknown experiencer of the phenomenon who surprisingly offers parallels to Stevens's account, indicative of a deeper absurdity of the phenomenon.

Chapter Six focuses exclusively on Stevens's theory of abstraction central to the poet's unique concept of self-disclosure, poetic function, and the human question wherefrom "supreme fiction"

---

[6] Richard M. Dolan, *UFOs for the 21st Century Mind: The Definitive Guide to the UFO Mystery*, new and exp. ed. (Richard Dolan Press, 2023).

evolved. Abstraction is defined as a methodological effort which pulls from within an idea of order sourced from without, hence a matter of poetic function. From abstraction develops an ethics of the imagination or "theoretical wisdom," which means to practice or apply the without; the wholly without, the outside of language itself within the tradition of rationalism. Despite fear of didacticism that is precisely what Stevens left us.

Chapter Seven revisits John Mack in the context of Stevens's theory, and the final chapter, which is lengthy, engages the concept of poetry itself, the irrational, philosophy, and the fine-grain aspects of Stevens's prose theory. It is most suitable for those interested in the academical takeaways specific to the phenomenon, modern philosophy, poetry, and its theory.

1

Five Poems of High Strangeness

> Nobody wants to be known as the person who has seen a UFO, so, if they see something anomalous, they usually choose the least unlikely explanation and leave it at that. The same is true of religious experiences.
>
> — Diana Walsh Pasulka[1]

In the early 1900s, a young Wallace Stevens lived and worked in New York City. In journals prior to 1905, he documents what I consider encounters with nonhuman intelligences (NHIs). The New York years he would reflectively call an "awakening" particular to a "return to poetry" around 1913.[2] By 1916, Stevens moved to Hartford, Connecticut, and less than a decade later Alfred P. Knopf published *Harmonium* (1923), the poet's most well-known collection of verse. "Uncollected Poems" of 1913–1915 as well as select poems from *Harmonium* offer insights into these encounters. We begin with "Hibiscus on the Sleeping Shores":

---

[1] Diana W. Pasulka, *American Cosmic: UFOs, Religion, Technology* (Oxford University Press, 2019), 79.

[2] Stevens had written poetry in years prior (1898–1910) but does not seem to commit to poetry in a decisive way until approximately 1913. Peter Brazeau, *Parts of a World: Wallace Stevens Remembered* (Random House, 1983), 7–9; 301.

> I say now, Fernando, that on that day
> The mind roamed as a moth roams,
> Among the blooms beyond the open sand;
>
> And that whatever noise the motion of the waves
> Made on the sea-weeds and the covered stones
> Disturbed not even the most idle ear.
>
> Then it was that that monstered moth
> Which had lain folded against the blue
> And the colored purple of the lazy sea,
>
> And which had drowsed along the bony shores,
> Shut to the blather that the water made,
> Rose up besprent and sought the flaming red
>
> Dabbled with yellow pollen — red as red
> As the flag above the old café —
> And roamed there all the stupid afternoon.[3]

Particular to "Hibiscus" is an anomalous object, the moth. While air ships were around in the early 1900s, what we find does not fit such a description. We are tasked to visualize something which "Rose up [...] and sought the flaming red" and the colors it dons "Dabbled with yellow," "red as red." How to interpret that "monstered moth" "Which had lain folded against the blue"? Metaphorically, "monstered" describes an indeterminate, moving object. Moreover, it's noiseless thus "Disturbed not even the most idle ear," which imparts an uncanny signature. I am impressed with the poet's stammering "that that" when declaring the object rose up "besprent" or covered with water. Equally, "The mind roamed as the moth roams" suggests that the mind is connected to this inchoate form. The question is whether a UFO or unidentified anomalous phenomenon (UAP) was observed

---

3 Wallace Stevens, *Collected Poetry and Prose* (The Library of America, 1997), 18.

by Stevens in the early twentieth century. Does it not accord to modern definitions of UAP, exhibiting transmedium capability, shape bifurcation, changing color, a lack of sound, rotor, and no visible means of propulsion?[4] I understand the leap required; it was one I had to make. Try to imagine this not as a poem.

> *There were clouds in the distance, I could hear the water on the sand and rocks. There was a silent object floating above the water. It was there for a long time, glowing, so I continued watching it. Strangely it dipped into the water and then reemerged and shot upward turning red.*

The above is an illustration. We won't know the precise nature of the experience itself. If Stevens did see a UFO, why bother with a poem? That is a simple question which concerns a complex subject. Thetically, Stevens unwittingly processed encounters with high strangeness through poetry. Many but not all UAP encounters leave experiencers with intermittent memories or none at all.[5] In other words, when the confoundment of a contactee is coupled with the fires of poetic imagination, the poet as experiencer becomes a possibility. Consider another example from *Harmonium*, titled "Palace of the Babies":

> The disbeliever walked the moonlit place,
> Outside of gates of hammered serafin,
> Observing the moon-blotches on the walls.
>
> The yellow rocked across the still façades,
> Or else sat spinning on the pinnacles,
> While he imagined humming sounds and sleep.

---

4 For readers new to ufology with interest in UFO/UAP "nuts-and-bolts" characteristics, see James Lacatski, Colm Kelleher, and George Knapp, *Inside the US Government Covert UFO Program: Initial Revelations* (RTMA, 2023).

5 This aspect of the phenomenon has been well documented. John E. Mack, *Abduction: Human Encounters with Aliens* (Scribner, 1994), 52–69.

> The walker in the moonlight walked alone,
> And each blank window of the building balked
> His loneliness and what was in his mind:
>
> If in a shimmering room the babies came,
> Drawn close by dreams of fledgling wing,
> It was because night nursed them in its fold.
>
> Night nursed not him in whose dark mind
> The clambering wings of birds of black revolved,
> Making harsh torment of the solitude.
>
> The walker in the moonlight walked alone,
> And in his heart his disbelief lay cold.
> His broad-brimmed hat came close upon his eyes.[6]

Once more, how might Stevens have reflected without the form of a poem?

> *A dream? What I have seen? Angels? Yellow shining on walls, objects spinning. Unreal. What was humming? I was there, walking? The building and the windows, strange windows, babies inside. Something in the dark, I remember, like feathers over feathers. Who to tell; who would believe me? Will they return? Too real to not be.*

"Babies" is otherworldly and cold. It bears the characteristics of a later "abduction phenomenon." There we find a glowing room from which "babies came." Does such signify neonate beings or a hybridization program? Considering the poet's shift from disbelief to belief, there is a strong notion of acceptance. Yet accepting what? Could the building be a craft which one enters "If in a shimmering room"? Why the hypothetical tone? Moreover, implied is a somnambulistic or trance-like state imagin-

---

6   Stevens, *Collected Poetry and Prose*, 61.

ing "humming sounds and sleep," which is a consistent theme throughout the oeuvre.

Was "Babies" too strange for critics? Despite being published in 1921, posthumous criticism such as Harold Bloom's *Poems of Our Climate* (1976) as well as *The Cambridge Companion to Wallace Stevens* (2007) do not engage it. Elanor Cook's Reader's Guide to Wallace Stevens (2007) which systematically interprets most of Stevens's poetry is quiet about it. Cook does mention "Hibiscus," focusing on "stupid afternoon," equating it with the poet being stunned, benumbed, or let down. Regarding "monstered moth," she views it part of Stevens's self-ideation "mind and monster."[7]

"Dolls", from the uncollected poems of 1913–1915 takes us further into the abduction thematic:

> The thought of Eve, within me, is a doll
> That does what I desire, as, to perplex,
> With apple-buds, the husband in her sire.
>
> There's a pious caliph, now, who prays and sees
> A vermeil cheek. He is half-conscious of
> The quaint seduction of a scented veil.
>
> Playing with dolls? A solid game, greybeards.
> Think of the cherubim and seraphim,
> And of Another, whom I must not name.[8]

A grown man sniffing a doll? Did he play with his sister's toys? Should we conclude a cuteish perversion with the inanimate? Unlike the moth sighting of "Hibiscus," the doll is an inchoate object within, a memory which the imagination apprehends. The doll moves into reflective thought and attains the status of Eve. It does what he desires yet drives him to question if he is

---

[7] Elanor Cook, *Reader's Guide to Wallace Stevens* (Princeton University Press, 2007) 44.

[8] Stevens, *Collected Poetry and Prose*, 517.

being deceived. The scent inhaled is laced in the veil. This veil conceals a face. Eve, once a doll with a vermilioned cheek, as if an apple, marks the appearance of the feminine archetype, the mother. The veil demarcates the unconscious from imaginary abstraction. With whom then does he play? There seems an ontological parity or gender neutrality at work as a second figure, the caliph, the Prophet of God appears. Thus follows the query: "Playing with dolls?" a retort to "greybeards" who play games. Greybeards? Perhaps Hárbarðr, or the trickster Loki, Hesperus the Morning Star, Venus? The poet thinks of "cherubim," "seraphim," and then "And of Another, whom I must not name." The Another?[9]

A late poem "The Well Dressed Man with a Beard" presents another inchoate form hovering above the house in the form of a halo. There we find an entity next to the poet in bed and the house is humming:

> After the final no there comes a yes
> And on that yes the future world depends.
> No was the night. Yes is this present sun.
> If the rejected things, the things denied,
> Slid over the western cataract, yet one,
> One only, one thing that was firm, [...]
> Out of a thing believed, a thing affirmed:
> The form on the pillow humming while one sleeps,
> The aureole above the humming house...
>
> It can never be satisfied, the mind, never.[10]

Had the doll(s) returned? What of the halo, that is, the "aureole" (areola)?[11] Replayed is a connection between mind and object

---

9 Stevens may be referencing W.G. Collingwood's illustration "Thor Threatened Greybeard," published c. 1908.
10 Stevens, *Collected Poetry and Prose*, 224.
11 "Lift characteristics" of reported UFOs are said to result in "halos" around the objects. Lacatski, Kelleher, and Knapp, *Inside the US Government Covert UFO Program*, 67, 109: "[M]agnetic fields developed by positive

not unlike metaphoric personifications already found. It comes to this: "Hibiscus," "Babies," "Dolls," and "Man with a Beard" carry an uncanny signature. Each integrates mind, object, and other beings. Such poems offer a benchmark from which I suppose three possibilities. First, Stevens has experiences with nonhuman intelligences and disguises them in poetry. With guile he reveals the weird masterfully. Fearing ridicule, he never tells a soul about it. Second, his imagination is prophetic. By coincidence he depicts happenings uncannily similar to the phenomenon decades before it exists in the public mind. Third, he cannot completely recall NHI encounters. Such are unwittingly revealed through a conflation of imagination and memory and unfold over time into his awareness. The first possibility, that Stevens was aware of NHI contact from his early years and disguises it as poetry seems plausible. The second I mostly reject; this inflates the poet's mystique and moves against Stevens's understanding of poetry; conversely, we cannot preclude such affecting the ego. The third possibility is the strongest. Stevens cannot completely recall NHI experiences yet has intermittent recollections. Such are initially involuntary and by circumstance configured within the poetic imagination.

How contact with nonhuman intelligence made its way into Stevens's poetry requires more than pointing out verse analogous to high strangeness. In order to understand how, "missing time" needs to be considered. Though an inexistent concept in Stevens's day, missing time was originally conceived by artist Budd Hopkins, who pioneered abduction regression hypnosis

---

electrical charges could explain many of the truly puzzling UFO observations: their silence; the lack of a sonic boom; their high accelerations and ability to make sharp changes in direction; clouds that form around them; halos which appear around them; the various colors emitted associated with the type of motion; radiation felt by observers; the disruption of electrical circuits; the spinning of magnetic compasses in their vicinity; their shapes; and the principles by which they could make interstellar trips." The authors quote a theory proposed by Eugene H. Burt, *UFOs and Diamagnetism: Correlations of UFO and Scientific Observations* (Exposition Press, 1970), formerly of Clark College, Atlanta.

in the 1980s. It was determined by observing subjects suffering mysterious fears and unreal memories. Hopkins defined it this way: "The events immediately before and immediately after the abduction" become,

> seamlessly joined leaving them with little or no sense of missing time. Many others may feel that there is really nothing more to remember about their encounter, most particularly in the cases where no physical traces exist [.... V]ery often the witness senses that something odd happened [...] and [...] simply does not want to find out what it was.[12]

Harvard psychiatrist John Mack, whom Hopkins trained in regression hypnosis, summarized missing time and the abduction phenomenon this way:

> Hopkins [...] documented [...] symptoms that indicate that abduction [...] might have taken place, as well as [...] sexual and reproductive episodes [...]. Temple University historian David Jacobs [...] refined the basic reported pattern of an abduction [...] such as manual or instrument examination, staring, and urological-gynecological procedures; secondary events, including machine examination, visualization, and child presentation; and ancillary events, [...] physical, mental, and sexual activities and procedures.[13]

While some of Mack's criteria are not found in Stevens's account, the poet may have believed missing time a function of the poetic muse if not "poetry itself."[14] Thetically his impetus to write poetry was an inadvertent recovery of lost conscious experience. Such informs an early quandary of belief which leads to an affirmation or "yes-saying" particular to the New York awak-

---

12 Budd Hopkins, *Missing Time: A Documented Study of UFO Abductions* (Richard Marek Publishers, 1981), 7–8.
13 Mack, *Abduction,* 451.
14 The use of "itself" is an important distinction that Stevens makes describing poetry's functionality. Stevens, *Collected Poetry and Prose,* 639, 824–25.

ening.[15] This recollection develops into his unique conceptualization of reality and the imagination.

Indications of recovered time might have been hinted at in Stevens's 1936 lecture "The Irrational Element in Poetry." There he divulges a "pretext for poetry" based upon a "poetic mechanism" or proclivity to detect happenings unique to "poetic sensibility."

> While there is nothing automatic about the poem, nevertheless it has an automatic aspect in the sense that it is what I wanted it to be without knowing before it was written what I wanted it to be, even though I knew before it was written what I wanted to do.[16]

This statement straddles question and affirmation. It seems as if the poet does not understand the source of his content yet abides by its truth. Would not the recall of missing time (without aid of another) be a novel experience itself, as if a predetermined yet new or an unknown familiar? Without therapeutic hypnosis, poetry would become a first draft of happenings once spirited away. Should this be believed, poetry concerns a revealing mechanism of self-disclosure, one which Stevens develops throughout his oeuvre. Stevens's "Yellow Afternoon," collected in Parts of a World (1942) informs the question of missing time further:

> Everything comes to him
> From the middle of his field. The odor
> Of earth penetrates more deeply than any word.
> There he touches his being. There as he is
> He is. The thought that he had found all this
> Among men, in a woman — she caught his breath —

---

[15] Stevens struggled with the Christian religion in the early 1910s, going so far as to throw away his Sunday school bible. Holly Stevens, ed., *Letters of Wallace Stevens* (University of California Press, 1981), 95–102, (nos. 124–29).

[16] Stevens, *Collected Poetry and Prose,* 784.

> But he came back as one comes back from the sun
> To lie on one's bed in the dark, close to a face
> Without eyes or mouth, that looks at one and speaks.[17]

Could "Yellow Afternoon" recollect being taken, as it were, yet not dressed in the characteristic horror of abductions decades later? For there we find a feminine form communicating telepathically with the poet in bed. As to Mack's summary, this being is indeed "staring" at Stevens. Missing time appears closer to the surface. For one, the poet is in a field. There he detects a penetrating odor. Next he's moved from daytime to nighttime, rather "he came back as one comes back from the sun." Precisely what the sun signifies is unknown. However, UFOs are often described as sun-like objects.[18] Present once more is a faceless face similarly concealed as it were in "Dolls." However, other attendant beings conflated with Eve appear within the context of desire and trickery, while neonates do not. If the being in "Dolls" seems ambiguously gendered, above there are no facial features.[19] In "Babies," "child presentation" is strongly suggested but resounds more of a dream state. I find these parallels too compelling to ignore, and yet, despite congruencies, missing time has limitations, writes Mack:

---

17 Ibid., 216.
18 Chris Bledsoe, a high-profile experiencer, describes his original encounter with UFOs as encountering sun-like objects. Danny Jones, "NASA's Forbidden Alien Study Finds Proof of Spiritual Beings | Chris & Emily Bledsoe," *YouTube,* December 4, 2023. https://www.youtube.com/watch?v=XmVQFX2Pp6o.
19 Cook identifies a "mysterious female figure, intensely apprehended" which "moves through several poems from this period." There are other poems where earth odor and movement take place aptly linked by Cook to Stevens's concept of the "poem of the earth." Cook, *Reader's Guide to Wallace Stevens,* 153, 156. Stevens remarks of "the poem of the earth" in "Imagination as Value" (1948). For Stevens, when this poem is written, it will "constitute the true prize of the spirit." Stevens, *Collected Poetry and Prose,* 730. Insofar as it concerns the phenomenon, the earth poem evokes ultraterrestial speculation, that NHI live in the mountains, earth, and oceans.

[T]he indicators of possible abduction used — such as seeing unusual lights, missing time, or a feeling of flying — may not [...] mean that an abduction has occurred [.... A]n even more serious difficulty [...] lies in the fact that we do not know what an abduction really is — the extent, for example, to which it represents an event in the physical world or to which it is an unusual subjective experience with physical manifestations. A still greater problem resides in the fact that memory in relation to abduction experiences behaves rather strangely [.... T]he memory of an abduction may be outside of consciousness until triggered many years later by another experience or situation that becomes associated with the original event. The experiencer [...] could be counted on the negative side of the ledger before the triggering experience and on the positive side after it.[20]

The poems could be a first draft of experiencer testimony originally confused as encounters with the muse. If so, this fits Mack's "negative side of the ledger," or what Stevens dedicated his later years to understanding through his theoretical prose particular to the concept of abstraction.

The Mandala

Did poetry help Stevens deal with contact experiences before the UFO phenomenon became part of the public imaginary? If that is to be believed, the oeuvre offers significant insight into the phenomenon's modern history. The fact is Stevens's verse is inundated with nonhuman and quasi-human forms, for example in "A Completely New Set of Objects":

> Shadows of friends, of those he knew, each bringing
> From the water in which he believed and out of desire

---

20 Mack, *Abduction*, 451.

> Things made by mid-terrestrial, mid-human
> Makers without knowing, or intending, uses.[21]

Such evoke a variety of beings known to UFO lore, whether extraterrestrial, ultraterrestial, interdimensional, or extratempestral.[22] Often we find strange interiors, levitation, humming sounds, telepathy, animate shadows, sequences of flying naked, and odors of earth. We also find craft, as in "Pieces," collected in *Transport to Summer* (1947):

> Tinsel in February, tinsel in August.
> There are things in a man besides his reason.
> Come home, wind, he kept crying and crying.
>
> Snow glistens in its instant in the air,
> Instant of millefiori bluely magnified —
> Come home, wind, he said as he climbed the stair —
>
> Crystal on crystal until crystal clouds
> Become an over-crystal out of ice,
> Exhaling these creations of itself.
>
> There is a sense in sounds beyond their meaning.
> The tinsel of August falling was like a flame
> That breathed on ground, more blue than red, more red
>
> Than green, fidgets of all-related fire.
> The wind is like a dog that runs away.
> But it is like a horse. It is like motion

---

21 Stevens, *Collected Poetry and Prose*, 307.

22 "Extratempestral" is a neologism that refers to a model developed and proposed by Michael Masters. Acknowledging his model's predecessors and through his own studies in biological anthropology, Masters proposes UFOs and aliens "may be our distant human descendants" capable of time travel. Michael Masters, *The Extratempestral Model* (Full Circle Press, 2022).

That lives in space. It is a person at night,
A member of the family, a tie,
An ethereal cousin, another milleman.²³

This features a classic UFO. As with "Hibiscus on the Sleeping Shores," an inchoate object with dazzling lights is integrated with the natural environment and fused with the mind. The poet longs for something as if recalling, as if desiring. He reminds himself reason is not the end of thinking. He cries and cries. "Come home" and that "blue millefiori," a clover shape found on a playing card; then, a thousand-leaved clover shape is "bluely magnified." There is a staircase ascended. An analogous scenario is found thirty years before in "Infernale" (1913–1914?).²⁴ The difference in "Pieces" is that the poet has entered the object by taking the stairs. "Infernale" carries a heavy mythological frame. There he sees a floating city with stairs he does not climb. Such hint at the progress of self-disclosure over the years which I suppose to be a transition between mythological framing, imagination, and deciphering screen memories. What cannot be ignored in "Pieces" is an object that "lives in space." An object familial hence an "ethereal cousin, another milleman," an object which "breathed on the ground" variating between blue and red, which strongly implies a landed saucer. It's all too similar to the classic UFO.²⁵

A robust psychological and intellectual account of the UFO comes from Carl Jung's *Flying Saucers*. Jung writes:

---

23 Stevens, *Collected Poetry and Prose*, 306–7.
24 Ibid., 518.
25 Blue and red color shifts indicate speed shifts in UFOs and is well understood in ufology, for example: *"Color Changes Associated With Flight Regimes:* The archives are full of reports of bright hovering objects changing color as they accelerate away […]. Each time it accelerated, its color changed to bright red, then gradually back to blue-white as it slowed and stopped." Lacatski, Kelleher, and Knapp, *Inside the US Government Covert UFO Program*, 110–11.

> The psychological experience [...] associated with the Ufo consists in the vision of the *rotundum,* the symbol of wholeness and the archetype that expresses itself in mandala form. Mandalas [...] usually appear in situations of psychic confusion and perplexity. The archetype thereby constellated represents a pattern of order which, like a psychological "viewfinder" marked with a cross or circle divided into four, is superimposed on the psychic chaos so that each content falls into place and the weltering confusion is held together by the protective circle.[26]

I suppose a potential mandala could be found in "Owl's Clover" (1935) and "Someone Puts a Pineapple Together" (1947). Of the latter, the mandala concerns a fruit on the table.[27] In "Owl's Clover," he will determine a statue, that "variable symbol," which ascends "To space?" In "Pineapple" we find "Apposites" at the "slightest edge, of the whole" and arrive upon an "Undescribed composition [...] Shiftings of an inchoate crystal tableau," concluding this way:

> An object the sum of its complications, seen
> And unseen. This is everybody's world.
> Here the total artifice reveals itself
>
> As the total reality. Therefore it is
> One says even of the odor of this fruit,
> That steeps the room, quickly, then not at all,
>
> It is more than the odor of this core of earth

---

26 C.G. Jung, *Flying Saucers: A Modern Myth of Things Seen in the Sky,* trans. R.F.C. Hull (Princeton University Press, 1978), 117. Emphasis in original.

27 "O juventes, O filii, he contemplates / A wholly artificial nature, in which / The profusion of metaphor has been increased. // It is something on a table that he sees, / The root of a form, as of this fruit, a fund, / The angel at the center of this rind, // This husk of Cuba, tufted emerald, / Himself, may be, the irreducible X / At the bottom of imagined artifice." Stevens, *Collected Poetry and Prose,* 693–94.

And water. It is that which is distilled
In the prolific ellipses that we know,

In the planes that tilt hard revelations on
The eye, a geometric glitter, tiltings
As of sections collecting toward the greenest cone.[28]

"Of Ideal Time And Choice" presents a variation of the mandala which is perplexing if not incoherent. There, "revolving crystalline" concerns temporal archaisms "Since thirty summers are needed for a year / And thirty years, in the galaxies of birth." Such is premised upon "thirty mornings are required to make / A day of which we say, this is the day / That we desired, a day of blank, blue wheels."[29] Implied is the wheel form of the mandala, which Jung notes is quantitative, qualitative, physical, and psychical.[30] Note also "the orator" who may well be "Another, whom I shall not name" found in "Dolls." Thus concludes "Of Ideal Time And Choice":

The orator will say that we ourselves
Stand at the center of ideal time,
The inhuman making choice of a human self.[31]

---

28 Ibid., 696–97.

29 Ibid., 697.

30 "The role that numbers play in mythology and in the unconscious [...] are an aspect of the physically real as well as of the psychically imaginary. They do not only count and measure, and are not merely quantitative; they also make qualitative statements and are therefore a mysterious something midway between myth and reality, partly discovered and partly invented. Equations, for instance, that were invented as pure mathematical formulae have subsequently proved to be formulations of the quantitative behaviour of physical things. Conversely, owing to their individual qualities, numbers can be vehicles for psychic processes in the unconscious. The structure of the mandala, for instance, is intrinsically mathematical." Jung, *Flying Saucers*, 103.

31 Stevens, *Collected Poetry and Prose*, 698.

THE POET AS EXPERIENCER

Ideal time surpasses common reason. The poet views human temporality from an exterior. To that consider Jung's summation: "What as a rule is seen is a body of *round* shape, disk-like or spherical, glowing or shining fierily in different colours, or, more seldom, a cigar-shaped or cylindrical figure of various sizes."[32] For Jung this concerns the collective unconscious "found in all epochs and in all places, always with the same meaning, and it reappears time and again, independently of tradition, in modern individuals as the 'protective' or apotropaic circle, whether in the form of the prehistoric 'sun wheel', or the magic circle, or the alchemical microcosm, or a modern *symbol of order,* which organizes and embraces the psychic totality."[33] The mandala: a floating halo above Stevens's house, the moth, the crystal palace. Do these not accord?

Are UFOs our own manifestations? If we accept Jung's ideations, could it be that Stevens generates a protective mandala as a consequence of commutation with NHI? That such psychic capacity was, in part, bestowed from his early years? Consider a sequence near the end of "Owl's Clover." Here the exterior of time is achieved by springing into space. From there a double sense of the self is made. One who is "hum-drum," a mere instrument, and another who witnesses his own life from above.

> The statue stands
> In hum-drum space, farewell, farewell, by day
> The green, white, blue of the ballad-eye, by night
> The mirror of other nights combined in one.
> The spring is hum-drum like an instrument,
> That a man without passion plays in an aimless way.
> Even imagination has an end,
> When the statue is not a thing imagined, a stone,
> The flight of emblemata through his mind,
> Thoughts by descent. To flourish the great cloak we wear
> At night, to turn away from the abominable

---

32 Jung, *Flying Saucers,* 19. Emphasis in original.
33 Ibid., 20. Emphasis in original.

> Farewells and, in the darkness, to feel again
> The reconciliation, the rapture of a time
> Without imagination, without past
> And without future, a present time, is that
> The passion, indifferent to the poets' hum,
> That we conceal?[34]

The question of concealment concerns NHI that Stevens attempts to integrate. In other words, a poet's hum *indifferent to the passion* must be unconcealed, for "The thing I hum appears to be / The rhythm of this celestial pantomime."[35]

The late poem "What We See Is What We Think" suggests developed commutation with NHI, declaring "what we think is never what we see," a strange reversal that begins with a clearer pronouncement of missing time:

> At twelve, the disintegration of afternoon
> Began, the return to phantomerei, if not
> To phantoms. Till then, it had been the other way:
> [...]
> Twelve meant as much as: the end of normal time,
> Straight up, an élan without harrowing,
> The imprescriptible zenith, free of harangue,[36]

"What We See" ends by describing a creature prior to a pyramid shape which may be the dog ear of a book he was reading:

> At the upper right, a pyramid with one side
> Like a spectral cut in its perception, a tilt
>
> And its tawny caricature and tawny life,
> Another thought, the paramount ado…
> Since what we think is never what we see.[37]

---

34 Stevens, *Collected Poetry and Prose*, 170.
35 "Landscape with Boat," in ibid., 221.
36 Ibid., 392–93.
37 Ibid., 393.

In his late prose Stevens was quite *confident* about the secular divine as found in "Two or Three Ideas" (1951): their gods and their annihilation he claims, were part of our own.

> To see the gods dispelled in mid-air and dissolve like clouds is one of the great human experiences. [...] It was as if they had never inhabited the earth. There was no crying out for their return. They were not forgotten because they had been a part of the glory of the earth. At the same time, no man ever muttered a petition in his heart for the restoration of those unreal shapes.[38]

Perhaps such statements solidify the poet's acceptance of his experiences. For the restoration of the unreal shape accords to Jung's "modern *symbol of order* which organizes and embraces the psychic totality."[39] Stevens did publish *Ideas of Order* (1935), suggesting such a role for poem and poetry.[40] Such "poetic order" sought to clarify what philosophic order and positivism denies. Replying to questions from *Partisan Review,* the poet offers his summation of these concepts:

> It seems that poetic order is potentially as significant as philosophic order. Accordingly, it is natural to project the idea of a theory of poetry that would be pretty much the same thing as a theory of the world based on a coordination of the poetic aspects of the world. Such an idea completely changes the significance of poetry. It does what poetry itself does, that is to say, it leads to a fresh conception of the world. The

---

[38] Ibid., 842. This is a perspective operative as early as 1922: "Addressing Clouds is an actual address to the clouds. The gloomy grammarians and funest philosophers are the clouds themselves. What could be simpler? Of course, it all depends on the point of view. People scent symbolism as if something of their own realism [...]. My things are all perfectly direct and mean just what they say even when that may seem a bit neither here nor there." Ibid., 938.

[39] Jung, *Flying Saucers,* 20. Emphasis in original.

[40] Stevens, *Collected Poetry and Prose,* 997.

sense of this latent significance exists. Many sensitive readers of poetry, without being mystics or romantics or metaphysicians, feel that there probably is available in reality something accessible through a theory of poetry which would make a profound difference in our sense of the world. The interest in the analysis and interpretation of poetry is the same thing as an interest in poetry itself. [...] The analysis and interpretation of poetry are perceptions of poetry.[41]

In this way, Stevens's thought operates as a revolution in scientific thought captured and rejected, as it were in Thomas Kuhn's understanding, within normal science. More broadly, as a poet Stevens does not fail to confront the epistemological obstacle by way of the poetic image intimately linked to the unconscious. Such comes by the "coordination of the poetic aspects of the world" or permissible expansion of reality by way of a poetic function, as "The great well of poetry is not other poetry but prose: reality. However it requires a poet to perceive the poetry in reality."[42] For Stevens, our knowledge is able to expand beyond materialism, naturalism, and the methodologies of rigid positivism. For the poet a celestial hum is informed by an external consciousness humans have yet to recognize; hence "the inhuman making a choice of a human self?" Part of this integration may well manifest UFOs, or what comes to be known as such. To this, Jung writes:

> The plurality of Ufos, then, is a projection of a number of psychic images of wholeness which appear in the sky because on the one hand they represent archetypes charged with energy and on the other hand are not recognized as psychic factors. [...] It is still in an archaic state, so to speak, where appercep-

---

[41] Ibid., 824–25. Poetic function and poetry itself are considered throughout this book, in particular in Chapter Six.

[42] Ibid., 919.

tions of this kind do not occur, and accordingly the relevant contents cannot be recognized as psychic factors.[43]

That UFOs may be generated by the mind perhaps explains what Stevens means by "poetic energy" and poetry's irrational element. In essence, correspondence with UFOs is not apparent or typically causal — they are necessarily lacking scientific explanation by sufficient causality. Jung continues:

> Moreover, it [apperception] is so trained that it must think of such images not as forms inherent in the psyche but as existing somewhere in extra-psychic, metaphysical space, or else as historical facts. When, therefore, the archetype receives from the conditions of the time and from the general psychic situation an additional charge of energy, it cannot, for the reasons I have described, be integrated directly into consciousness, but is forced to manifest itself indirectly in the form of spontaneous projections. The projected image then appears as an ostensibly physical fact independent of the individual psyche and its nature. In other words, the rounded wholeness of the mandala becomes a space ship controlled by an intelligent being.[44]

Here an excess of energy lies latent. Whatever substance manifests through *psyche materialis*[45] at base, would be a general substance, elemental and without reason; hence irrational. The materialized poem, as a thing, is embossed with facets of an inchoate object of the abstract, otherwise forms of the formless. Such forms are transliterated into human language from an incommensurable exterior — a conscious substance without its local cognizance. A poet with fidelity to the instant records such glimpses and goes about their willful muse-chasing. Only

---

43 Jung, *Flying Saucers*, 29.
44 Ibid.
45 Loosely this means the integration of the mental and physical in regard to an eidetic content of consciousness. Implications of the soul, *psyche*, are intentional.

in review would they find traces of metalanguage, hints of an arcane logic otherwise unwitnessed at the moment of a compulsive act.[46] Thus Mack's problematization of missing time or what "could be counted on the negative side of the ledger before the triggering experience and on the positive side after it" I find congruent with Stevens's insistence on poetic energy, one he triggers willfully when engaging the world.[47] Thetically, Stevens generates his own UFO through an extrapsychic linkage discovered in his first awakening. This informs the poet's consideration of an "absolute object" similar to Jung's apotropaic circle (a similar form generated by Dante through the signifier of Beatrice).[48] Yet I hesitate to take Jung's prognostications to the fullest.

---

[46] Jacques Vallee claims to have coined the term "metalogic," which is somewhat disingenuous, as it is linked to Heinrich Scholz's 1931 work *"Abriss der Geschichte der Logik" (Outline of the History of Logic)* and Alfred Tarski's *The Concept of Truth in Formalized Languages* (1933), and associated with Kurt Gödel's "incompleteness theorems" (1931). Conversely, the latter have the term attributed, whereas the former initiates the term. Nonetheless, metalogic is grouped with metalanguage, which determines subjective consciousness is "meta" to the formal system and offers a critical insight that such formalism precludes by its own rules. Vallee did not coin this but is the first to apply it to the phenomenon. For our concerns, this insight is poetry itself, as Vallee partially conceded in the past. His current position on poetry and theory is unknown. Jacques Vallee, *Alien Contact Trilogy*, vol. 1: *Dimensions: A Casebook of Alien Contact* (Anomalist Books, 2003), 136.

[47] This was made clear in the prose text *The Noble Rider and the Sound of Words* (1942), as with *The Irrational Element in Poetry* (1936).

[48] Perhaps Dante finds what may be his own apotropaic circle in *The New Life:* "Ego tanquam centrum circuli, cui simili modo se habent circumferentiæ partes: tu autem non sic." "I am the centre of a circle, equidistant from all points on their circumference; but you are not." Dante Alighieri, *The New Life*, trans. J.G. Nichols (Herperus, 2003), 74.

2

Credible Rhetoric

> I do not for a moment mean to indulge in mystical rhetoric,
> since for my part, I have no patience with that sort of thing.
> That the unknown as the source of knowledge, as the object of
> thought, is part of the dynamics of the known does not permit
> of denial. It is the unknown that excites the ardor of scholars,
> who, in the known alone, would shrivel up with boredom.
> We accept the unknown even when we are most skeptical.
> We may resent the consideration of it by any except the most
> lucid minds; but when so considered, it has seductions more
> powerful and more profound than those of the known.
> — Wallace Stevens[1]

When Wallace Stevens passed away in 1955, UFO sightings began an uptick. More importantly, he had come of age at the turn of the twentieth century. Despite remaining active in his final decade, there are no remarks on the 1947 "flying saucer" crash at Roswell or Kenneth Arnold's well-publicized sighting near Mount Rainier that June. Beyond words, Stevens's experiences have no corroborating witnesses, images, or material evidences. Therefore, reading the oeuvre as contactee testimony requires

---

1 Wallace Stevens, "The Irrational Element in Poetry," in *Collected Poetry and Prose* (The Library of America, 1997), 791.

differentiation between probable experiences and desire for false positives. This is not new to ufology, which has as many views as there are researchers. Among the most well-known is historian Richard Dolan, whose decades-long research reads consistent, trustworthy, and earnest.[2] Thus, when Dolan notes "there were many [...] startling sightings of the 1920s and 1930s [...] lost to us forever," the question turns to the timeframe of Stevens's actual experiences and how these might inform the historical arc of the modern phenomenon.[3]

According to Dolan, strange airships observed in the skies of Chicago and Aurora, Texas, in early April 1897, resembled what a "few people claimed to see [...] two cigar-shaped objects joined together and with great wings. From time to time it was illuminated by the rays of two giant searchlights."[4] The improbability of such technologies Dolan emphasizes as well: witness accounts of nonhuman pilots which appeared in local newspapers and defy explanation to this day. It turns out Stevens described airships to his wife in June 1910: "In the afternoon, I may go out to Hempstead Plains where there are a number of air-ships — (bi-planes) to be on exhibition. Air-ships are thrilling beyond description — and when you are home again I must try to take you to see a flight. That sight of Curtiss coming down the river from Albany remains vivid."[5] His description of Glenn Curtiss's historic flight on May 29, 1910, is not what I would consider a UFO sighting. Weirdly the 1910 entry jokingly remarks of cigars after reference to said craft, yet what is required is humor and care: we cannot force Stevens's words to mean something they don't. To this writes Dolan: "For several days in January,

---

2 The difficulty with evidence is a long story, one interwoven with governmental deception, NHI deception, and the changing capacity of documentation. Dolan covers the degrees of evidence in his book. Richard M. Dolan, *UFOs for the 21st Century Mind: The Definitive Guide to the UFO Mystery*, new and exp. ed. (Richard Dolan Press, 2023), 294–300.

3 Ibid., 111.

4 Ibid., 106.

5 Holly Stevens, ed., *Letters of Wallace Stevens* (University of California Press, 1966), 168 (no. 174).

1910, there were airship sightings in Chattanooga, Tennessee. Thousands of people rushed out of their homes in broad daylight to see a huge, white, cigar-shaped object, plainly in view, flying around above the city. This went on for several days in a row, until the so-called airship was captured. It was a 15 footlong home-made balloon set aloft as a prank."[6] An intense study of poetry discloses in strange ways — this I can attest to — however the above should not satisfy the most generous apologist. What Stevens remarks of in 1910 is ironic but not a coded sighting and by example distinguishes his rhetorical tone.

It comes to this: I propose missing time and NHI contact occurs in and around New York City between 1900 and 1904. Thenceforward Stevens is increasingly driven to chase his muse. As the verse develops, he unwittingly recovers lost conscious experience through poems composed up to 1916, his last year in New York and the final year of a first "awakening."[7] Outside of the verse, five journal entries strongly suggest contact with NHI did occur in the years 1900–1904, and these are the focus of the following two chapters. From them, I attempt to determine the question of missing time. Then Stevens was in his early twenties, unencumbered by fame, marriage, and career. Eventually the publisher Alfred Knopf collects Stevens's poems to publish in *Harmonium,* and most appear to have been written from 1915–1923.[8] After the 1923 publication, Stevens dives deep into careering and will not reemerge as a poet until an expanded version of *Harmonium* is published in 1931.[9] The likelihood that poems were written throughout his hiatus is decent. If he had

---

6 Dolan, *UFOs for the 21st Century Mind,* 109.

7 Stevens held company with the avant-gardians of the so-called "Arensburg Circle," which encouraged his poetic output. At this time, he published poems in little magazines and met Marcel Duchamp. Peter Brazaeu, *Parts of a World: Wallace Stevens Remembered* (Random House, 1983), 7, 11.

8 Poems were added in later versions of *Harmonuim.* Originally, sixty-eight poems were collected in the first printing. Elanor Cook, *Reader's Guide to Wallace Stevens* (Princeton University Press, 2007), 29.

9 In 1926 Stevens's hiatus from poetry meant that he threw himself into work. However, his life pace contributed to blurred vision and high blood pressure by the late 1920s. Brazeau, *Parts of a World,* 243–47.

additional contact experiences, he may well have suppressed them or they remain unknown. Or worse, these accounts might have been destroyed posthumously as were some of his letters, unintentionally or otherwise.

Poems studied in the previous chapter span 1913–1947. They are meant to illustrate the arc of Stevens's awareness and eventual self-disclosure. If these were preceded by unwitting recollections of missing time conflated with the muse, they do not reveal when and where Stevens's first contact occurs. The fact that *Harmonium* was published in 1923 does not mean contact occurs in the 1920s (which Dolan notes as a crucial decade). Examining the oeuvre, it is clear ideas were replayed, expanded, and developed over forty years. If contact occurs and concludes before 1910, how much of his later content was based from seed memory? After all, a memory is already subjected to imagining, thus transforming through every iteration. Conversely, Stevens may have sustained commutation with NHI.

Outside of high strangeness the young Stevens surrounded himself with the energies and personas of New York City in the early 1900s. It's likely self-doubt or insecurities came into play at one point or another. Additionally, Stevens experienced a particular shattering. For example, in a letter from 1906, Stevens "meditates" on suicide.[10] A strong thread of misanthropy in the entries of this period and an eventual disconnection from his religious upbringing underscore the point.[11] Conversely, misanthropy and suicide are not the subject of the poems we have access to from this period. They already remark of otherworldly matters. In mid-1908, Stevens dedicates "A Book of Verses" to his then future wife. Judging the exuberance expressed to Elsie

---

10 "Somehow, in this season, I like to get my pipe going well, and meditate on suicide. It is such splendid melancholy, and, mixed with a little beer and whiskey—divine." Stevens, *Letters of Wallace Stevens,* 90 (no. 113).

11 "Last night was house-cleaning [...]. I went through my things [...] and threw away a pile of useless stuff. How hard it is to do it! One of the things was my Bible. I hate the look of a Bible. This was one that had been given to me for going to Sunday-school every Sunday in a certain year. I'm glad the silly thing is gone." Ibid., 102 (no. 129).

in letters, one assumes his most intimate core was laid bare. Two poems from "A Book of Verses" suggest contact experiences. In fact, they are similar to themes replayed again and again throughout his oeuvre in decades to come, the first being poem VIII, "Winter Melody":

> I went into the dim wood
>   And walked alone.
> I heard the icy forest move
>   With icy tone.
>
> My heart leapt in the dim wood
>   So cold, so bare —
> And seemed to echo, suddenly,
>   Old music there.
>
> I halted in the dim wood,
>   And watched, and soon,
> There rose for me — a second time —
>   The pageant moon.[12]

Is this an unremarkable poem? After all it's about the moon so, what's new? But why does the moon rise a "second time—"? What role do the em dashes play? For there are no apparent clauses to follow. Why is the beauty of this moon preceded by "Old music there"? This suggests a deeper stratum. While this does not really recall "The Palace of the Babies" or achieve its uncanny world, it does resound a similar scenario. As does untitled poem XIV from "A Book of Verses":

> There is my spectre,
> Pink evening moon,
> Haunting me, Caliban,
> With its Ariel tune.

---

12 Stevens, *Collected Poetry and Prose*, 502–3.

> It leads me away
> From the rickety town,
> To the sombre hill
> Of the dazzling crown.
>
> Away from my room,
> Through many a door,
> Through many a field
> I shall cross no more.
>
> After man, and the seas,
> And the last blue land,
> At the world's rough end,
> If, perchance, I should stand
>
> To rest from long flight —
> Pale evening moon,
> I should never escape
> That wild, starry tune.[13]

Here two Shakespearean characters, Caliban and Ariel, earth brute and air spirit, haunt the poet who is brought to a "sombre hill" upon which a "dazzling crown" is found. "Crown" appears many times in the oeuvre (literally and more so as figure). We do have to stretch a bit if we compare crown to the haloes associated with UFOs. However, it's notable that the poet has flown out of his room through many doors and across the land. Here a tentative relationship to "Yellow Afternoon" and later poems such as "Landscape with Boat" seem possible.[14] Intriguingly, poem XIV features a "spectre" or visitor which is equivocally

---

13 Ibid., 505.
14 "Yellow Afternoon" follows a poem "Variations on a Summer Day" as collected in *Parts of a World* (1942) which may also link to this early verse. Such remarks of "sub-music like sub-speech, / A repetition of unconscious things," and then "Star over Monhegan, Atlantic star, / Lantern without a bearer, you drift, / You, too, are drifting, in spite of your course; / Unless in the darkness, brightly-crowned, / You are the will, if there is a will, / Or

the moon which leads the poet away. This moon is at first pink, then pale as something "I should never escape."[15] Is it banal to suppose the crown a craft or its artifact? That Caliban is a haggard dwarf and Ariel a faceless Eve-being, supposedly feminine (who for Shakespeare was androgynous, but whom Stevens considered a man)?

On January 17, 1909, Ariel appears again as Stevens writes to Elsie.[16] There our poet is complaining about city life and his solitude:

> [B]ooks make up. They shatter the groove, as far as the mind is concerned. They are like so many fantastic lights filling plain darkness with strange colors. I do not think I complained for myself, but for the letters. Do you remember — (if it matters)? — I like to write most when the young Ariel sits, as you know how, at the head of my pen and whispers to me — many things; for I like his fancies, and his occasional music. —[17]

Note again the em dashes — if this seems pedantic I must insist that to a poet it matters greatly. And, certainly, what to make of "fantastic lights filling plain darkness with strange colors?" If Stevens is recovering contact experiences by 1909, it is obvious he equates it with the muse; if not, then a being of one order or

---

the portent of a will that was, / One of the portents of the will that was." Stevens, *Collected Poetry and Prose*, 212–13.

15 Levitation is a feature of abduction or contact experience, for example: "Cases of uncontrolled levitation or gravity effects have been reported in connection with UFOs. In one case, which took place in 1954 in the French countryside, a man who was coming back from the fields with his horse had to let go of the bridle as the animal was lifted several feet into the air — a dark, circular object was flying fast over the trail they were following." Jacques Vallee, *Dimensions: A Casebook of Alien Contact* (Alien Contact Trilogy 1) (Anomalist Books, 2003), 206–7.

16 The problem with analyzing Elsie's letters is the fact she destroyed many of them. Overall, editorial choices by the poet's daughter, Holly, seemingly exclude unsavory content. Stevens, *Letters of Wallace Stevens*, xiv.

17 Ibid., 123 (no. 144).

another. No doubt Ariel is a name he gives it. If Stevens's stoic confidence has long baffled critics, I ask the reader to consider how they would feel if divinity chose you? *I know something you would never understand, I am a true poet, a most real poet.* Who would you tell, if not the person you were to spend the rest of your life with? That Elsie listened might have been enough to want to be with her, someone, anyone. In a journal from 1902 he will term an owl encountered outdoors "Ariel-owl." Though mentioned a few times in the oeuvre, Ariel is a significant figure, if only as a name that place-holds an elusive being recounted four decades later in "The Planet on the Table" (1951):

> Ariel was glad he had written his poems.
> They were of a remembered time
> Or of something seen that he liked.
>
> Other makings of the sun
> Were waste and welter
> And the ripe shrub writhed.
>
> His self and the sun were one
> And his poems, although makings of his self,
> Were no less makings of the sun.
>
> It was not important that they survive.
> What mattered was that they should bear
> Some lineament or character,
>
> Some affluence, if only half-perceived,
> In the poverty of their words
> Of the planet of which they were part.[18]

---

18 Stevens, *Collected Poetry and Prose*, 450.

Poetry, Theory, and Self-Disclosure

A closer examination of poetry, philosophy, science, and technology are the subject of the final chapter. However, I feel compelled to set an emphasis on the historical development, basic concepts, and the peculiar quality of Stevens's realizations. In other words, if Richard Dolan has not yet considered poetry, that is entirely understandable. Nonetheless, he highlights the need for "philosophical and investigative issues," which Stevens undoubtedly provides. When Dolan asks, "how ordinary objects and events might fool us, and how they differ from 'true UFOs,'" questions about "mind-to-mind communication" and "human consciousness" have already been exampled.[19] In prose Stevens considered the interrelation between imagination and reality at length. If required is the discernment between "fact from fiction, and legitimate issues from fear-mongering or fantasy-peddling" in an age of information saturation,[20] Stevens believed fiction was closer to the truth, which is a matter that complicates our relation to official facts. Stevens's theoretical lecturing was yet another addition to his first draft of experiencer testimony from the early twentieth century, one which unsurprisingly faced barriers ufologist deal with today. Thus, if disclosure remains the ultimate prize, how likely are we to trust the official view? At the height of our "smart" or "intelligent" world system, are we not already eclipsed by a seeping cynicism — that everything is illusion, a psyop or general deception?

Disclosure was an individual process through a poetic function, Stevens theorizes.[21] In simple terms, certain poets are com-

---

19 Dolan, *UFOs for the 21st Century Mind,* 27.
20 Ibid.
21 For example, "A Discovery of Thought" declares: "The first word would be of the susceptible being arrived, / The immaculate disclosure of the secret, no more obscured." Stevens, *Collected Poetry and Prose,* 459. Prose such as "Three Academic Pieces" retrospectively instructs what the poetry revealed, "What our eyes behold may well be the text of life but one's meditations on the text and the disclosures of these meditations are no less a part of the structure of reality." Ibid., 689.

pelled to write at the moment of inception. For Stevens this concerns what is encountered *without,* which unlocks something *within.* A parallel to this would be Dante Alighieri's *La vita nuova,* or *The New Life.* Originally written in 1295, it describes the poet's overwhelming obsession with Beatrice Portinari. Beatrice, as she is known throughout his oeuvre, was a real human being who died five years before *The New Life* was written. Dante barely knew her; however, he wanders around medieval Florence seeking her out. Throughout, Dante describes fantastical experiences with the divine which, in one instance manifests as an apotropaic circle. A similar obsession pervades the oeuvre of Stevens. Already in Chapter One we observed instances of a divine muse buried within memory. With regard to external reality, does Stevens seek analogous, triggering scenarios? This is, I suppose, the case with "Owl's Clover," a poem with far too many signifiers of UFO lore to be denied: dwarves, orbs, out-of-body, telepathy, and space travel.

Thetically, Stevens's cognizance of NHI unfolds inadvertently, through his own method and imaginative will; unofficially for himself, by himself, which evolves toward a "poetry of thought" or the attempt to develop a quasi-divine knowledge by way of an "absolute object." The oeuvre offers two possibilities how self-disclosure might have evolved. First is that NHI contact ends in the 1910s and the poet is left with an inscrutable mystery suppressed subconsciously. He spends the rest of his life recovering experiences with no true awareness of contact. Careful reading dispels this position. Experiences of high strangeness in the early years were recovered first on an imaginary level, recollected yet unrecognized. These commutations were partially cognized before the 1930s, resulting in a second awakening of the early 1930s. The second awakening concerns a willful attempt at commensurability with nonhuman beings. Thus, the first "awakening" of the New York years 1900–1916 unfolds dramatically by the early 1930s.[22] As a second awakening takes form, Stevens's

---

22 Stevens read Sigmund Freud's the *Interpretation of Dreams* (1897) and, later, *The Future of an Illusion* (1927). There is no indication Stevens was

theory defines its primary quandary as "abstraction," which inevitably leads to the concepts of "supreme fiction."[23] A hiatus from poetry in the years 1923–1933 follows Harmonium. While the Great Depression affected everyone, he may have sought what some fail to do — become normal. Nonetheless by 1934, the Stevens family settles in their permanent residence in Hartford. At the time his daughter was ten years old and he'd been married for a quarter century. Thereafter, notoriety as a major American poet would be established.[24]

At times, Stevens's theory reads like a coping mechanism, a coming to terms with his imagination. He waxes heroically as if he were poetry's redeemer. He remarks that poetry concerns an ordering function and implies, at first, that he is its unwitting savior. If some contactees go on to form religions or adopt the profiteer's pose this was not the case for Stevens. We find an unadulterated path of self-revelation through an exterior point of view, one removed from charlatanism, profiteering, or hysteria. The fact that Stevens read part of "Owl's Clover" within his first lecture "The Irrational Element in Poetry" (1936) underscores the point. This poem is not only intensive experiencer testimony, but also displays the poetic function of self-disclosure; what may well be Stevens's greatest innovation. That his earliest theorization of NHI encounters was read to an academic audience at Harvard is significant, as the phenomenon had no such history in the way we know it today. Examining *Letters*, he anticipated the lecture "the way one must look forward to

---

aware of Carl Jung, despite his study of French translator and critic Charles Mauron (1899–1966), who used psychoanalysis to investigate aesthetics. Stevens read Mauron's *Aesthetics and Psychology* (1935), which mentions Jung but once.

23 Some critics suggest Stevens's entrance into academic circles meant he wanted to avoid life, his wife; that poetry and theory were escapism. Others claim he was ensconced politically thus motivated to recover a fading reputation.

24 Stevens was awarded the National Book Award twice: in 1950 for *The Auroras of Autumn* (1950) and in 1954 for *Collected Poems* (1954). In 1955 he received the Pulitzer Prize.

one's first baby."²⁵ Appraising rhetoric one finds aphoristic revelations and irrational apologetics. Poetry he determines to be a process of subjectification, informed by a natural mystery he was at times reluctant to explain. For example, "The Irrational Element" ends with a disquieting prognostication regarding "poetic energy" and that "It will be time enough to adopt a more systematic usage, when the critique of the irrational comes to be written, by whomever it may be that this potent subject ultimately engages."²⁶ Precisely what "potent subject" refers to, and what, for that matter, a critique of the irrational means, was not clearly conveyed. Could it have meant, literally: "a face / Without eyes or mouth, that looks at one and speaks."²⁷ That messages were imparted to him telepathically? Might critique mean a task of poetry informed by NHI — first as a means of self-disclosure, then to implement their advices? Does this critique encourage us to develop a knowledge of intelligences beyond or beside our own? Is it a call for spiritual or physical evolutionary change? Or does he mean by critique our own terrestrial intelligences attempting to appropriate NHIs for their own *arcana imperii*? However one may receive it, provided was a novel account of commutations with "the intelligence" itself.²⁸

As to the motive for theory, there are questions we may never answer. Stevens was well-to-do financially. He had an executive career in the insurance industry, so one is right to question why he bothered with academia.²⁹ Indeed, *Letters* reveals an antagonism peaking by the early 1940s. Then the poet knows better

---

25 Stevens, *Letters of Wallace Stevens*, 313 (no. 352).
26 Stevens, *Collected Poetry and Prose*, 792.
27 Ibid., 216.
28 Stevens does not directly reference "the intelligence" in "The Irrational Element in Poetry," but prior to its composition he contemplates the distinction in letters to Ronald Lane Latimer. See Chapter Six.
29 In a letter to Hi Simons, Stevens admits he was not satisfied with "The Irrational Element in Poetry," remarking on "captious people" who seemed to have not received it well. He expressed the same feelings about "The Noble Rider and the Sound of Words." Throughout the years, Stevens reiterated key ideas in other lectures. Stevens, *Letters of Wallace Stevens*, 392 (no. 429).

than philosophers who'd heard him out before. Directly challenging the "official view of being," Stevens delivers his "intimidating thesis" insisting on "poetic fact" over "absolute fact," propounding a "credibility" of supreme fiction as the "triumph over the incredible."[30] He declares that a poet's "unreal" transforms reality by virtue of its source in a real, "the imagination is man's power over nature"; a refutation of scientific naturalism and an affirmation of panpsychist ideation.[31] Despite his perceived adversaries, Stevens's ambition to penetrate the academic shield continued throughout the 1940s. He delivered more lectures reflectively termed "contributions" to "a theory of poetry." By the decade's end he's tasked to collect them into a standalone volume, *The Necessary Angel* (1951). In its "Introduction" he considers theory a "most ardent" ambition[32]; and it's notable that he excludes "The Irrational Element."[33]

Theoretical concepts are also developed in the primary tenants of *Notes Toward a Supreme Fiction* (1942). This includes questioning of whether "it must be human," as stated in a letter from 1954 less than a year before his death.[34] As he entered his final years (1951–1955), what became the uncollected prose was more amicable to philosophers than in the past. There, the poet sought to illuminate poetry and philosophy in terms of shared ideas, hence a "poetry of thought."[35] Broadly speaking, Stevens's reverence for earth's sanctity was emergent in his younger years,

---

30 Stevens, *Collected Poetry and Prose*, 680.

31 Ibid., 921.

32 Ibid., 639.

33 This seems to be derived from literary critic I.A. Richards and applied to William Carlos Williams in the preface to the latter's *Collected Poems 1921–1931*. It is the first instance of a theoretical device I could find in prose. Stevens, *Collected Poetry and Prose*, 771.

34 In a 1954 letter to critic Robert Pack, Stevens writes "For a long time, I have thought of adding other sections to the NOTES and one in particular: *It Must Be Human*. But I think that it would be wrong not to leave well enough alone." Stevens, *Letters of Wallace Stevens*, 863–64 (no. 955).

35 Stevens, *Collected Poetry and Prose*, 855. "A Collect of Philosophy" (1951) was rejected for publication by Paul Weiss, an academic philosopher he corresponded with and quotes.

which reads similar to that of future experiencers exposed to scenes of apocalypse by their captors. At times one finds antihumanist and contranaturalist perspectives. There are ideations about belief, that everything is a fiction we believe in; that even if we deny it, beliefs are extensions of reality. If that implies a front running of "simulation theory" or an "alien-self" conception, it's driven by an intrapersonal, spiritual confrontation. This concerns "the intelligence" and deception, hence illusion and fulfilment, precisely the ethical dilemma at the core of poetry's theory.

Radio and Region

When it comes to the contemporary UFO, media technologies as well as literature have influence. And yet Wallace Stevens experienced an America different from the later twentieth and early twenty-first centuries. His childhood and teenage years took place in the late 1800s, in a world where books had a privileged role. At the turn of the century, he was twenty-one. By the time he published *Harmonium* (1923) he was in his mid-forties. In the early 1920s, radio adoption was approximately one percent and by early 1930s receivers would appear in a slight majority of American homes. By the late 1930s the technology was domestically widespread. Stevens was critical of media pumped through the radio and held disdain for the effect it had on people's sensibilities.[36] Encountering a radio would have been a rare occurrence before 1910, yet it is clear that Stevens believes doing so deadens the connection to the divine. The poem "A Thought

---

[36] In the early 1930s "Stevens spent a good deal of his time listening to the radio and, later, the phonograph as he accumulated an impressive library of classical records, many of them imported. He also read a good deal at this time, as well as becoming an avid gardener [...]. But apparently it was not a time or an atmosphere conducive to creativity. His energy, in this period between the ages of forty-four and fifty-two, went largely into his work at the insurance company." Stevens, *Letters of Wallace Stevens*, 242–43.

Revolved," collected in *The Man with the Blue Guitar* (1937) examples aversion to the "mechanical optimist":

> A lady dying of diabetes
> Listened to the radio,
> Catching the lesser dithyrambs.
> So heaven collects its bleating lambs.
>
> Her useless bracelets fondly fluttered,
> Paddling the melodic swirls,
> The idea of god no longer sputtered
> At the roots of her indifferent curls.[37]

By the early 1940s, radio was a matter of an "ever-enlarging incoherence."[38] Such was based on a lack of "any authority except force, operative or immanent. What has been called the disparagement of reason is an instance of the absence of authority. We pick up the radio and find that comedians regard the public use of words of more than two syllables funny."[39] If not himself to what authority is he referring? Stevens's polemic wants to exceed what English critic I.A. Richards similarly termed "self-dissolving introspection."[40] For our poet it means to diminish an "awareness of the goings-on of other people's minds" into *"merely as goings-on."*[41] A lack of intimacy seems central to his criticism: "We lie in bed and listen to a broadcast from Cairo, and so on. There is no distance. We are intimate with people we have never seen and, unhappily, they are intimate with us."[42] What then was the preferred intimacy? What drove him to pro-

---

37 Stevens, *Collected Poetry and Prose*, 171.
38 Ibid., 652.
39 Ibid.
40 Ibid., 653.
41 Ibid., 654.
42 Ibid., 653. This view emerges in journals of the early 1900s: "[Y]esterday I went to Morristown and back. My brain was like so much cold pudding. First, I loathed every man I met, and wanted to get away, as if I were some wild beast. People look at one so intimately, so stupidly." Stevens, *Letters of Wallace Stevens,* 86 (no. 107).

ject such criticism and insist, as he did, on poetic order? By the late 1940s the polemic approaches the level of a rant:

> So, too, if, to our surprise, we should meet one of these morons whose remarks are so conspicuous a part of the folklore of the world of the radio — remarks made without using either the tongue or the brain, spouted much like the spoutings of small whales — we should recognize him as below the level of nature but not as below the level of the imagination. It is not, however, a question of above or below but simply of beyond.[43]

What accounts for "beyond" will be conceptualized by Stevens as "region," a placeholder term for access to language's exterior regarding poetry's "true subject." In his prose of the late 1940s, he revisits a maxim formalized a decade prior regarding distinctions between the "true subject" of poetry and the "poetry of the subject." His example was Picasso.

> Picasso has a subject, a subject that devours him and devastates his region. Possibly a better illustration would be one that is less intimidating. Whether we like it or not, all of us who have radios or who go to the movies hear a great deal of popular music. Usually this is music without a subject. You have only to tabulate the titles of the songs you hear over a

---

43 Stevens, *Collected Poetry and Prose*, 688. It's noteworthy "above, below, beyond" is similar to Carl Jung's conception of correspondence. Writes Jung: "The animate world is the larger circle, man is the 'Limbus minor,' the smaller circle. He is the microcosm. Consequently, everything without is within, everything above is below. Between all things in the larger and smaller circles reigns 'correspondence' (*correspondentia*), a notion that culminates in Swedenborg's *homo maximus* as a gigantic anthropomorphization of the universe." C.G. Jung, "Parcelsus the Physician I," in *The Collected Works of C.G. Jung*, vol. 15: *Spirit in Man, Art, and Literature*, ed. and trans. Gerhard Adler, eds. Herbert Read, Michael Fordham, and William McGuire (Princeton University Press, 1983), 9273.

short period of time to convince yourself of this. The titles are trivial, catchy, trite and silly.[44]

The distinction between the true subject and the fanciful parallels his denunciation of an inorganic wasteland, filled with dead air and even deader brains. But that does not tell us Stevens's true subject. What devoured or devastated his region? Why would a self-styled, private poet be concerned enough to inform audiences of his distaste?

The use of "region" gains in complexity overtime. In the oeuvre it suggests the potential of actual reality, reprising the transition of Ideas in the philosophies of Plato and Aristotle.[45] This can be found in "Life on a Battleship" which begins with the poet supposing to "seize" and thus "build / A single ship, a cloud on the sea, the largest / Possible machine, a divinity of steel."[46] Yet the poet becomes neither captain nor ship itself; rather, they assume a supreme position of no position, a matter of parts and whole — from beyond.[47] Here region concerns a "sceptre" which moves from "constable to god, from earth to air, The circle of the sceptre growing large / And larger as it moves, moving toward / A hand that fails to seize it."[48] It enters into a soliloquy with the "High captain" where the poet is told of "grand / Simplifications approach but do not touch / The ultimate one, though they are

---

44 Stevens, *Collected Poetry and Prose*, 716.
45 In "Snow and Stars" one may "remove it to his regions." Ibid., 108. When asked in a 1939 interview for *Partisan Review,* if his poetry reflects any allegiance, nationalism, or region, Stevens replied, "Unquestionably and notwithstanding the fact that I indulge in a good deal of abstraction, I do not regard my poems as mainly an expression of myself, nor as modern in the sense in which that unpleasant commonplace is so frequently used." Ibid., 804.
46 Ibid., 198.
47 The battleship is not the true subject. That is, "Life on a Battleship" is not about battleships, as such would be the poetry of the subject which contradicts his basic concept. Because the poetry of the subject concerns battleships, the true subject (which is paramount) concerns cosmic intimacy; a desire to grasp the captain within.
48 Stevens, *Collected Poetry and Prose,* 201.

THE POET AS EXPERIENCER

parts of it."⁴⁹ This drama arrives at reflective speculation: "If the sceptre returns to earth, still moving, still / Precious from the region of the hand, still bright / With saintly imagination."⁵⁰ Does the captain serve as an authority? Are they flying in space? Here the poet remarks of the captain's *"Regulae mundi"* or rules of the world before returning to earth commenting "… That much is out of the way."⁵¹

The hand is an abstractor of actual things, it turns the radio dial for that electromechanical search engine. A potential hand is something else. It extends and rescinds from some metaphysical region; out of and in to time. By the imagination such hand is infinite. It needs no algorithmic predication, ego, nation, or ideological program (see "The Hand as a Being"⁵²). What is the potent hand trying to grasp, the captain, an arcane secret, or the magic wand held by some being? The hand is in at least two places at once; the hand is metaphor itself; it dips between conscious and subconsciousness. One may suppose it abstracts from a region; what provides and rescinds interdimensionally. Thus "the region of the hand" attains actuality as mental phenomenon. How else to account for the poem's end?

> It must be the hand of one, it must be the hand
> Of a man, that seizes our strength, will seize it to be
> Merely the centre of a circle, spread
> To the final full, an end without rhetoric.⁵³

---

49 Ibid.
50 Ibid.
51 Ibid.
52 Ibid., 242.
53 Ibid., 201.

3

Owl's Palace

> Not the ocean of the virtuosi
> But the ugly alien, the mask that speaks
> Things unintelligible, yet understood.
>
> — Wallace Stevens[1]

A Private Palace

In June 1900, a young Wallace Stevens completes a three-year program at Harvard and moves into a small apartment in New York City. He covers political campaigns for the *New York Tribune*, takes in the city, attends the theater, and experiments with playwriting. By the spring of 1901, the then twenty-one-year-old wants to quit the *Tribune* and become a writer. His father, who supports him financially, refuses, insisting he study law. By the fall of 1901, Stevens concedes and enrolls at New York University. During this time, a significant encounter with nonhuman intelligence seems to have taken place in February 1901, right after Stevens rents "a hall bed-room" in a house on 124 East 24th Street. On February 7, he journals one of his adventures:

---

1 Wallace Stevens, *Collected Poetry and Prose* (The Library of America, 1997), 126.

This afternoon I took a walk from the house up to Central Park and through it. I got to the Park after sunset, although the Western horizon was still bright with its cold yellow. The drives were white with snow and at times the air was quite full of the cheering sound of sleighbells. I hurried through the Mall or Grand Alley or whatever it is; went down those mighty stairs to the fountain; followed a path around the lake, and came to a tower surrounded with a sort of parapet. The park was deserted yet I felt royal in my empty palace. A dozen or more stars were shining. Leaving the tower and parapets I wandered about in a maze of paths some of which led to an invisible cave. By this time it was dark and I stumbled about over little bridges that creaked under my step, up hills, and through trees. An owl hooted. I stopped and suddenly felt the mysterious spirit of nature—a very mysterious spirit, one I thought never to have met with again. I breathed in the air and shook off the lethargy that has controlled me for so long a time. But my Ariel-owl stopped hooting + the spirit slipped away and left me looking with amusement at the extremely unmysterious and not at all spiritual hotels and apartment houses that were lined up like elegant factories on the West side of the Park. I crossed to Eighth-ave., and in a short time returned to the house.[2]

Those familiar with UFO lore might have raised an eyebrow. What to make of the maze of paths leading to "an invisible cave," "a very mysterious spirit" which he "thought never to have met with again" and vanished "lethargy" that had "controlled me for so long a time"? What about the "Ariel-owl" and a presence which "slipped away" after a joyful reunion? Note: "I felt royal in my empty palace."

Central Park was built atop an African American settlement named Seneca Village. In the early 1900s it was approximately sixty years old. The path Stevens likely took from his room on

---

2 Holly Stevens, ed., *Letters of Wallace Stevens* (University of California Press, 1966), 50 (no. 55).

East 24th Street was via Fifth Avenue. His exit from Central Park was on Eight Avenue or the westside of Manhattan. On foot it would have been an eight-mile walk taking approximately three hours. Depending on how long he spent there, he may well have been gone much longer. Inside Central Park, "The Mall" that he hurried through leads to two different fountains. It's likely he reached the Angels of the Waters fountain at the bottom of those "mighty stairs" of Bethesda Terrace. From there, Stevens circled "The Lake" probably along West Drive, though he may have crossed "Bow Bridge." The latter is unlikely as he encountered a "tower" with a "parapet" (likely Belvedere Castle) before finding the "maze." Either way he is sure to have entered "The Ramble," a heavily treed series of interlocking passages. The "invisible cave" he discovers is almost certainly Indian Cave, later named Ramble Cave, thus an actual cave with a rather dark history.[3] That a young man encounters an owl upon a hill in Central Park, which spans over 800 acres, is not itself a remarkable occurrence. It's almost a given that Central Park in 1901 had animals within it. He finds it in "The Ramble," which to this day hosts most of the park's wildlife, including owls.

The motive for the young Stevens's adventure may well be prosaic. In the spring months of 1901, he is unsatisfied working at the *Tribune* and desires a life of adventure and letters. In March, his father denies him that. Strangely he did not journal again until August 1902 (or these journals, as with other letters, were posthumously destroyed). May we surmise the owl and "mysterious spirit of nature — a very mysterious spirit, one I thought never to have met with again" is simply a wanton young man desperate for spiritual reconnection? If only that, his journals are standard *Bildungsroman* material.

Indeed, a year and a half prior Stevens journaled about skies, the moon, flora, and fauna mixed with occasional philosophical vamps. For example, on August 1, 1899, he writes an early

---

3   BookwormHistory, "The Ramble Cave," *Atlas Obscura,* October 2, 2015, https://www.atlasobscura.com/places/the-ramble-cave-new-york-new-york.

version of one of his key maxims: "I'm completely satisfied that behind every physical fact there is a divine force. Don't, therefore, look <u>at</u> facts, but <u>through</u> them."[4] In early 1900, he questions if a career in literature is a wise choice or even possible. Already his insistence on the imagination used spiritually means to connect if not transform reality beyond tedium. Might we suppose on February 7, 1901, the experience with the owl is heightened or elevated through the framework of an already existent view? For the moment the owl's presence ceases, the young poet finds the scene "extremely unmysterious and not at all spiritual," regarding the "hotels and apartment houses that were lined up like elegant factories on the West side of the Park." This more or less aligns with the limit of the imagination's extreme achievement, which "lies in abstraction," as Stevens propounds decades later.[5]

I have played the skeptic to demonstrate careful reading. Conversely, such accounts are not mere musings — they are Stevens's reality. He has a concept for encountering the divine, which suggests familiarity with the strange. This could mean that Stevens's Central Park encounter was not the first. Moreover, "staging" by an NHI is a possibility. Staging is an anesthetizing of resistance or fear by NHI. It involves the simulation of local reality in order to deceive a contactee so the beings can go about their business. Experiencers often remark of humming sounds or noisy occurrences similar to poems we have already considered.[6] In *Abduction: Human Encounters with Aliens* (1994), John Mack offers an interesting parallel:

> [T]he aliens appear to be consummate shape-shifters, often appearing initially to the abductees as animals — owls, eagles, raccoons, and deer are among the creatures the abductees have seen initially — while the ships themselves may be

---

4 Stevens, *Letters of Wallace Stevens,* 32 (no. 35).
5 Stevens, *Collected Poetry and Prose,* 728.
6 "[H]umming sounds, buzzing noises, and sounds compared to the swarming of bees are commonly reported as the auditory perception associated with a UFO." Jacques Vallee, *Alien Contact Trilogy,* vol. 1: *Dimensions: A Casebook of Alien Contact,* (Anomalist Books, 2003), 201.

disguised as helicopters or, as in the case of one of my clients, as a too-tall kangaroo that appeared in a park when the abductee was seven. The connection with animal spirits is very powerful for many abductees.[7]

What concerns "alternative physical realities" Mack finds "one of the more interesting mysteries." One abductee's story "abounds with rooms, like the dining room [...] which are not quite the actual rooms of his house, and landscapes with caves and trails that are not there upon later searching."[8] In the case of "Catherine," staging concerns "'goofy' tricks [...] appropriate to her level of consciousness at the time. Once [...] through the staging theatricals, the room was returned to its original state and Catherine was told to sit on a small, cold metal chair."[9] UFO historian Richard Dolan reports that NHIs "place a screen memory into the mind of the abductee, often an unusual owl, deer, or other type of animal."[10] Recounting Budd Hopkins's *Missing Time* (1981) — "probably the single most important book in all of abduction research" — Dolan notes abductions are not random: "most abductees were taken multiple times for years and years, starting in their youth, if not infancy. Abduction was a recurrent, albeit largely hidden, feature of their lives."[11] Asserted is that NHIs operate on their own agenda, "that abductions are a widespread operation [...] presumably for something considered to be of great importance to these other beings," on which Dolan opines that "even if not necessarily evil [...] it is easy to see why alien entities would wish to conceal what was going on from humanity."[12]

---

7 John E. Mack, *Abduction: Human Encounters with Aliens* (Scribner, 1994), 34–35.

8 Ibid., 292–93.

9 Ibid., 172.

10 Richard M. Dolan, *UFOs for the 21st Century Mind: The Definitive Guide to the UFO Mystery: New and Expanded Edition* (Richard Dolan Press, 2023), 361.

11 Ibid., 362.

12 Ibid.

In the foreword to Mike Clelland's *The Messengers* (2020), Dolan affirms that the owl seems to extend "screen memories" and concerns "real owls." Clelland's book features accounts which "suggest that owls play a role in a number of alien or UFO encounters." In certain instances, people "have been directed to see UFOs because of the actions of owls." In chapter four, "An Owl and a Flying Orb," Clelland introduces an experiencer named JB, according to whom an orb appeared and which he sought to pursue:

> The owl was facing its head at me, and then redirecting its head towards the sky and moving its head around in a circular motion, or, circular like fashion. I kept going between the sky, and owl, searching for the orb again. The owl kept repeating this noise and because of this I ended up losing the orb in the sky. The owl had flown away right before I could see the orb again.[13]

In an entry from October 13, 1902, Stevens reports an eager return to a wooded area around Palisades, Yonkers, which begins this way: "Apollo + I tripped it through the rainy woods […]. I raced to beat him to the tope of one hill […] and I won."[14] (Apollo means poetry.) Upon arriving, writes Stevens:

> Overhead the moon shone from a strange azure of its own creating. Spirits seemed everywhere—stalking in the infernal forest. The wet sides of leaves glittered like plates of steel; night-birds made thin noises; tree-frogs seemed conspiring; an owl chilled the clammy silence. But pooh! I discovered egg-shells-sure sign of a man + his wife + a child or two, loafing in my temple. How fine, though, was the mystery of

---

13 Mike Clelland, *The Messengers: Owls, Synchronicity and the UFO Abductee* (Beneath the Stars Press, 2020), 82.
14 Stevens, *Letters of Wallace Stevens*, 61 (no. 67).

everything except the damned egg-shells! How deep + voluble the shadows![15]

In both entries an owl marks the moment where spiritual experience begins and, as with the February 7, 1901 entry, ends. In both, heightened experience returns to normal. Here the "palace" of Central Park, in which he felt "royal" is a "temple." Specific to February 7 and implied in the October 13 experience is the possibility of *"abaissement du niveau mental."* Carl Jung analyzed the UFO testimony of Orfeo Angelucci accordingly:

> After these revelations Angelucci felt exalted and strengthened. It was "as though momentarily I had transcended mortality and was somehow related to these superior beings." When the lights disappeared, it seemed to him that the everyday world had lost its reality and become an abode of shadows.
>
> On July 23, 1952, he felt unwell and stayed away from work. In the evening he took a walk, and on the way back, in a lonely place, similar sensations came over him as he had felt on May 23. Combined with them was "the dulling of consciousness I had noted on that other occasion", i.e., the awareness of an *abaissement du niveau mental,* a state which is a very important precondition for the occurrence of spontaneous psychic phenomena. Suddenly he saw a luminous object on the ground before him, like an "igloo" or a "huge, misty soap bubble." This object visibly increased in solidity, and he saw something like a doorway leading into a brightly lit interior. He stepped inside, and found himself in a vaulted room, about eighteen feet in diameter. The walls were made of some "ethereal mother-of-pearl stuff."[16]

---

15 Ibid., 62 (no. 67).

16 C.G. Jung, *Flying Saucers: A Modern Myth of Things Seen in the Sky,* trans. R.F.C. Hull (Princeton University Press, 1978), 114.

THE POET AS EXPERIENCER

Recall: "The walker in the moonlight walked alone," and "If in a shimmering room, the babies came." Recall: "the spirit slipped away and left me looking with amusement at the extremely unmysterious and not at all spiritual hotels and apartment houses." Consider Angelucci's misty soap bubbles and Stevens's blue millefiori as found in "Pieces." Note that in both experiences a craft appears along with a staircase, which is then ascended. What about the noises? Recall from Stevens's October 13, 1902 entry: "How deep + voluble the shadows!" This word "voluble" means that *shadows* talk. Anyone who has spent time in the woods at night understands an analogous experience; however, I am drawn back to "The Palace of the Babies" and the night's personification: "It was because night nursed them in its fold."[17] Such shadow-talk changes from monotonic to dialogic throughout the verse. First as desire mired in dreaming, for example, in the early verse "Sunday Morning," "What is divinity if it can come / Only in silent shadows and dreams?"[18] Then a complex consideration of "motionless sound" found in "Sad Strains of a Gay Waltz" where the poet dances with strange beings. When said desire is sated, found is "a mode / Of revealing desire and is empty of shadows."[19] This culminates with "The epic of disbelief" and a possible confrontation:

> Some harmonious skeptic soon in a skeptical music
>
> Will unite these figures of men and their shapes
> Will glisten again with motion, the music
> Will be motion and full of shadows.[20]

Observe the dance and the role of shadows, emptied and filled.[21] This being comes in shadow and dream.

---

17 Stevens, *Collected Poetry and Prose*, 61.
18 Ibid., 53.
19 Ibid., 100.
20 Ibid., 101.
21 Elanor Cook makes an apropos connection to the use of "Hoon" in this poem, referring back to "Tea at the Palaz of Hoon." Hoon is the vision-

"Chocorua to Its Neighbor," a poem of the 1940s, strongly suggests NHI cognizance had developed further. First it seems Stevens experiences an NHI based within a mountain which is eventually equivocated to himself replaying the mind–monster dyad of "Hibiscus on the Sleeping Shores." "Chocorua" details the complexity of such willful relation. Verses III, XVIII, XX, XXVI describe an evolved role of shadows: "this prodigious shadow, who then came / In an elemental freedom," of "True transfigurers fetched out of the human mountain, / True genii for the diminished, spheres, / Gigantic embryos of populations, / Blue friends in shadows"[22] — to which he addresses the reader as the mountain itself: "Now, I, Chocorua, speak of this shadow as / A human thing. It is an eminence," concluding, "In my presence, the companion of presences / Greater than mine, of his demanding, head / And, of human realizings, rugged roy...."[23]

In verses IX and X Stevens remarks on "silver-shaping size" and "silver shapeless, gold encrusted size."[24] What to make of the genii and the spheres, the silver shape which is both shapeless and apparently changing in size? Has he found the Jinn? And of course, "embryos" recounting the neonate as found in "Palace of the Babies" and "Dolls". Stevens deploys a neologism "fortelleze": "This is their captain and philosopher, / He that is fortelleze, though he be / Hard to perceive and harder still to touch." What is going on here? Furthermore, captain of what? Elanor Cook's *A Reader's Guide to Wallace Stevens* defines "fortelleze" to possibly mean foretelling. Cook's emphasis on -eze converts it to 'ease'; however, I think a likelier interpretation would be a type of speaking, as if Chinese or Milanese; sugges-

---

ary personification of the poet, writes Cook: "A mountain-top as a place of vision is a familiar topos," thus analyzing "Hoon, a visionary self for Stevens, is now identified as a solitary, hardly surprising for someone of his gifts." Elanor Cook, *Reader's Guide to Wallace Stevens* (Princeton University Press, 2007), 62, 90.

22 Stevens, *Collected Poetry and Prose,* 264, 266.
23 Ibid., 267–68.
24 Stevens, *Collected Poetry and Prose,* 265.

tive of telepathy "hard to perceive" by a being "harder still to touch."[25] Another oddity of Mt. Chocorua correlates with the proximate location of the famous abduction story of Betty and Barney Hill on September 19–20, 1961.[26] Finally, Cook's surmising that "rugged roy" was a reference to "royal" for me implies "my royal palace" or that temple regarding the owl encounters of the early years.[27]

Let us move from the shadows back to owls. In *Stories from the Messengers,* Clelland summarizes owl encounters in the following ways:

> 1. Owls are alarm clocks […] they are here to wake us up. But […] to what?
>
> 2. Owls are an archetype. They are a symbol, an image stored deep within humanity's genetic memory bank. It's as if there are hidden meanings locked away within our grand shared consciousness, and the owl is a key.
>
> 3. Owls are here to announce initiation […]. Owls often seem to show up just before the arrival of a UFO, as if to announce an impending ritual.
>
> 4. Owls are a totem of the transformational experience. Seeing a UFO can transform someone. I've spoken to a lot of people who've seen a strange craft in the sky, and in that moment their entire definition of reality is altered. I've also spoken to people who have had owl sightings at such highly charged

---

25 Cook, *Reader's Guide to Wallace Stevens,* 177.
26 The Hills traversed the mountainous area on Route 3. From Twin Mountain, Cannon Mountain, Old Man of the Mountain and eventually Indian Head approximately 50–60 miles from Mt. Chocorua. *Wikipedia,* s.v. "Barney and Betty Hill incident," https://en.wikipedia.org/wiki/Barney_and_Betty_Hill_incident.
27 Cook, *Reader's Guide to Wallace Stevens,* 177. Consider also once more, from February 1901: "I felt royal in my empty palace."

moments that it transformed their lives. But a transformation into what?[28]

If the owl already plays a strong role in Stevens's oeuvre prior to "Owl's Clover," it certainly does so after. Says "On the Adequacy of Landscape": "The little owl flew through the night, / As if the people in the air / Were frightened and he frightened them, / By being there," concluding, "So that he that suffers most desires / The red bird most and the strongest sky— / Not the people in the air that hear / The little owl fly."[29] Note the "red bird," as if an orb. Note also the noiseless fliers which the people in the air hear. Owls. This poem collected in *Parts of a World* (1942) is part of a sequence of verse with owls, such as "Woman Looking at a Vase of Flowers" and "Landscape with Boat." In "Woman Looking at a Vase of Flowers" the owl is personified, marking a transformation between "human" and "inhuman":

> It was as if thunder took form upon
> The piano, that time: the time when the crude
> And jealous grandeurs of sun and sky
> Scattered themselves in the garden, like
> The wind dissolving into birds,
> The clouds becoming braided girls.
> It was like the sea poured out again
> In east wind beating the shutters at night.
>
> Hoot, little owl within her, how
> High blue became particular
> In the leaf and bud and how the red,
> Flicked into pieces, points of air,
> Became-how the central, essential red
> Escaped its large abstraction, became,
> First, summer, then a lesser time,
> Then the sides of peaches, of dusky pears.

---

28 Clelland, *The Messengers*, 142.
29 Stevens, *Collected Poetry and Prose*, 221–22.

> Hoot how the inhuman colors fell
> Into place beside her, where she was,
> Like human conciliations, more like
> A profounder reconciling, an act,
> An affirmation free from doubt.
> The crude and jealous formlessness
> Became the form and the fragrance of things
> Without clairvoyance, close to her.[30]

Consider an excerpt from the late poem "The Owl in the Sarcophagus," dedicated to Stevens's long-term friend and advocate Henry Church, who had recently passed away. It seems Stevens delves into things he's never shared with Church though may have wanted to:

> Without a voice, inventions of farewell.
> These forms are not abortive figures, rocks,
> Impenetrable symbols, motionless. They move
>
> About the night. They live without our light,
> In an element not the heaviness of time,
> In which reality is prodigy.[31]

There are many extrapolations to make regarding the "prodigy" of reality, something which lives "without our light," without the weight of time; something motionless which moves as had sound in "Chocorua to Its Neighbor." At base, Clelland's owl conceptualization has an unusual symmetry: Could the owl's sarcophagus signify aspects of our own hidden consciousness? Does it remark of an interface used by beings outside of human time?

---

30 Ibid., 224–25.
31 Ibid., 371.

"If These Were Theoretical People"

Stevens's grand poem "Owl's Clover" (1935) features an orb which plays a significant role. There we are presented with "a wandering orb upon a path grown clear."[32] Could this be our "red bird"? That "sprawling portent" which moves "High up in heaven" from "the crow's perspective of trees / Stands brimming white, chiaroscuro scaled / To space. To space? The statue scaled to space."[33] Those conversant in UFO phenomena might have raised all three eyebrows. Nonetheless, what becomes of the portent? "The portent would become man-haggard to / A race of dwarves,"[34] such as in poem III, preceding this portent as "The shallowest iris on the emptiest eye. / The future must bear within it every past," for "The portent may itself be memory; / And memory may itself be time to come / And must be, when the portent, changed, takes on / A mask up-gathered brilliantly from the dirt."[35] Note the poem informs us that memory *is a portent.* And note that the anomaly then presents itself, "steps forth, priestly in severity, / Yet lord, a mask of flame, the sprawling form / A wandering orb."[36] Is he then "Without clairvoyance, close to her"?[37]

That the statue emerges from the ground and ascends "To space. To space?" suggests anomalous abilities not dissimilar to those mentioned in "Hibiscus on the Sleeping Shores" or "Pieces." Critical reception of "Owl's Clover" shadows the poem by an emphasis on political meanings. While Stevens doesn't avoid addressing such, this poem has strong parallels to his experiences in Central Park, namely the Angel of the Waters

---

32 Ibid., 169.
33 Ibid.
34 Ibid., 170. Jacques Vallee has compiled numerous accounts of dwarf sightings throughout human history. Jacques Vallee, "Chapter Three: The Secret Commonwealth," in *Passport to Magonia: From Folklore to Flying Saucers* (Daily Grail Publishing, 1969).
35 Stevens, *Collected Poetry and Prose*, 169.
36 Ibid.
37 Ibid., 225.

THE POET AS EXPERIENCER

fountain and equally those "deep, voluble shadows." Stevens conceived the statue in "Owl's Clover" as a "variable symbol" which could signify whatever to whomever. For me it carries several key signifiers of the phenomenon.[38] Moreover, I think it linked to an earlier poem "In a Garden," composed in 1909:

> Oh, what soft wings shall rise above this place,
> This little garden of spiced bergamot,
> Poppy and iris and forget-me-not,
> On Doomsday, to the ghostly Throne of space!
>
> The haunting wings, most like the visible trace
> Of passing azure in a shadowy spot—
> The wings of spirits, native to this plot,
> Returning to their intermitted Grace!
>
> And one shall mingle in her cloudy hair
> Blossoms of twilight, dark as her dark eyes;
> And one to Heaven upon her arm shall bear
> Colors of what she was in her first birth;
> And all shall carry upward through the skies
> Odor and dew of the familiar earth.[39]

Stevens wrote often about eyes. Alien eyes have been described by modern experiencers as having a profound communicative effect including telepathy or the imparting of coldness — other accounts are of familial ties. There are eighteen places in "Owl's Clover" that mention eyes and over one-hundred instances in Stevens's entire oeuvre. "Yellow Afternoon" offers a rare and explicit instance of a face without eyes, whereas "In a Garden" presents "dark eyes."[40] In poem IV of "Owl's Clover" Stevens speculate on what he faces:

---

38 Ibid., 590.
39 Stevens, *Collected Poetry and Prose,* 508–9.
40 Ibid., 508. Mack, *Abduction,* 314–16. "From all of this turmoil, confusion, and misunderstanding, powerful, sometimes transcendent connections form between human beings and the alien visitors that appear to grow

> If these were theoretical people, like
> Small bees of spring, sniffing the coldest buds
> Of a time to come — A shade of horror turns
> The bees to scorpions blackly-barbed, a shade
> Of fear changes the scorpions to skins
> Concealed in glittering grass, dank reptile skins.[41]

Consider "If these were theoretical people,": the use of "if" indicates a thetic question which suggests they are not. Here voluble shadows are shade. Does it recount what the journal had: "The wet sides of leaves glittered like plates of steel; night-birds made thin noises; tree-frogs seemed conspiring; an owl chilled the clammy silence?" Here I note the only instance of anything reptile. Insects feature in a handful of instances. From poem V "Sombre Figuration" of "Owl's Clover":

> A mumbling at the elbow, turgid tunes,
> As of insects or cloud-stricken birds, away
> And away, dialogues between incognitos.
> He dwells below, the man below, in less
> Than body and in less than mind, ogre,
> Inhabitant, in less than shape, of shapes
> That are dissembled in vague memory
> Yet still retain resemblances, remain
> Remembrances, a place of a field of lights,
> As a church is a bell and people are an eye,

---

out of mutual need. For the abductees the relationships seem to serve a desire for self-knowledge and for a less egocentered kind of cosmic love that takes them beyond their bodies to a sense of oneness with the creative Source. As we shall see, the depth of knowledge and understanding reflected in the beings' great eyes is an important aspect of this connection. For the beings the contact sems to fulfill a hunger for nurturance and eroticism, lost or never before known, even for the experience of physicality itself. The actuality and power of the relationship can be so intense that it seems to override ontological considerations, such as 'where' all this is taking place." John E. Mack, *Passport to the Cosmos* (White Crow Books, 1999), 267–68.

41 Stevens, *Collected Poetry and Prose*, 166–67.

A cry, the pallor of a dress, a touch.

It is difficult to ignore the poet who observes "the man below" as if out of body or flying. Then the "remembrances" and the "field of lights." If "Owl's Clover" divulges NHI contact, it summons a thinking about the absurd in art, namely surrealism. Is this merely intentional style? Stevens was not a surrealist poet and his position on the matter he made clear in "The Irrational Element in Poetry" (1936):

> There are, naturally, charlatans of the irrational. That, however, does not require us to identify the irrational with the charlatans. I should not want to be misunderstood as having the poets of surrealism in mind.[42]

Stevens describes poetry in terms of a poet's need or "a dynamic cause for the poetry he writes." Thus, of the surrealist poets and "their dynamic effort […] means 'they make other forms obsolete' however they "in time, will be absorbed […] and become part of the process of give and take of which the growth of poetry persists."[43] Poems are apparatuses of self-disclosure and those "who seek for the freshness and strangeness of poetry […] do so because of an intense need."[44] Need and desire for what? In my analysis, poems retain and "disclose" consciousness withheld, they are part of a subjectification process. Genre is otherwise an articulation of an intelligence which discloses individuation between the "true subject," which concerns an orderly acquiescence to "poetic mechanism," and "poetic sensibility." Such allows the true to come forth even if unwittingly.

Owls concern missing time in Stevens's early journals. This forms the basis of Stevens's testimonial evidence for a relationship with the phenomenon which intensifies in first decades of the twentieth century. If I find Stevens's Central Park expe-

---

42 Ibid., 791.
43 Ibid.
44 Ibid.

riences to be genuine NHI encounters, there are other examples of staging. References to rooms or palaces can be found in "Parochial Theme," more extraordinarily "Dezembrum," "Certain Phenomena of Sound," "Less and Less Human," "O Savage Spirit," and several accountings in the long and complex "An Ordinary Evening in New Haven." In the early verse some notable instances are also found in "Piano Practice at the Academy of Holy Angels," "Six Significant Landscapes," and of course "Palace of the Babies." Some accounts concern potential UFO, shape-shifting, strange females, and other post-existential affirmations of divinity and desire. The reader is encouraged to undertake their own reading.

4

The Blue Gods of Organismus

> His spirit grew uncertain of delight,
> Certain of its uncertainty, in which
> That dark companion left him unconsoled
>
> For a self returning mostly memory.
> Only last year he said that the naked moon
> Was not the moon he used to see, to feel
>
> (In the pale coherences of moon and mood
> When he was young), naked and alien,
> More leanly shining from a lankier sky.
>
> — Wallace Stevens[1]

Fairies

A journal entry from September 4, 1902, reveals agitation. There is an increasing distance from spiritual experience. The study of law compresses a desire and Stevens contemplates "Organismus" as a "one." He praises this "scientific" concept but also eschews it:

---

1   Wallace Stevens, *Collected Poetry and Prose* (The Library of America, 1997), 119–20.

> [I]f I were a materialist I might value it. But only last night I was lamenting that the fairies were things of the past. The organismus is truck — give me the fairies, the Cloud-Gatherer, the Prince of Peace, the Mirror of Virtue — and a pleasant road to think of them on, and a starry night to be with them.[2]

A few years removed from the owls of 1901 and 1902, we find a beleaguered lawyer to-be. Nonetheless, in June of 1904, Stevens passes the bar examination. What to make of a want for fairies? It may regard a few months prior to the bar when, on April 18, 1904, he ventures to Tomkins Cove and writes of fairies and little people once again:

> God! What a thing blue is! It is one of the few things left that bring tears to my eyes (or almost). It pulls at the heart with an irresistible sadness. It seems as if it were the dusk of the lost Pleiades, as if it were a twilight where any moment the fairies might light their lamps. Faith, that point about the fairies is only too true. It has set my bladder rattling, as witness.[3]

Stevens then journals a poem.

> *Time.* Any absolutely cloudless day.
> *Place* etc. On a high hill. Stevens stands on the alert and his large ear picks out these sounds twenty miles away. —
> *Persons.* One of the fairies singing to his harp:
>
> Be thou my hood
> Bright columbine
> And thou my staff
> O, green, green vine

---

[2] Holly Stevens, ed., *Letters of Wallace Stevens* (University of California Press, 1966), 60 (no. 64).

[3] Ibid., 72 (no. 89).

> I would pursue
> The beam that brings
> So sweet a hope
> Of sweeter things
>
> And rest me there
> On its soft star,
> To hear it chime —
> Songs from afar.[4]

What to make of literature's influence? For most of his life, Stevens's media was exclusively print and one could assume conflations of outdoor experiences with literature and youthful desire. Might this be the case with regard to the entry of April 18, 1904? Careful reading is required. Note "faith, that point of the fairies is only too true" goes to the core of ufology, namely Jacques Vallee's heralded analyses in *Passport to Magonia* (1969). Vallee's cataloguing of NHI encounters explores Walter Wentz's *The Fairy-Faith in Celtic Countries,* Its Psychological Origin and Nature (1909).[5] As this book did not exist during Stevens's earliest suspected contact, we may want for Stevens's source; *Edmund Spencer's The Faeirie Queene* (1569) is a strong probability, however. Furthermore, Stevens may have been referring to Randolph Rogers "The Lost Pleiad" or references made in the bible.[6]

In addition to literature's support for a materialist skepticism, let us attend to the known facts of Stevens's epic journey. A young man, presumedly fit, claims to have walked forty-two miles in

---

[4] Ibid. This poem is revisited a few years later, it seems under the title "In April" collected in *The Little June Book* (1909). Stevens, *Collected Poetry and Prose,* 513–14.

[5] Jacques Vallee, *Passport to Magonia: From Folklore to Flying Saucers* (Daily Grail Publishing, 1969), 72–73.

[6] Stevens may have used biblical knowledge as a reference or framing to interpret or make sense of encounters. Though not writing about Stevens, Diana Pasulka theorizes this well. See Diane W. Pasulka, *American Cosmic: UFOs, Religion, Technology* (Oxford University Press, 2019), 2–3, 9, 14–15.

a single day "from Undercliff Avenue to Fort Montgomery."[7] While possible, it requires a very strident and steady pace. He woke at 4am, had breakfast, then crossed either the Harlem or the Hudson river by 7am; a distance of 2.5 miles if the Hudson, and less than a mile if the Harlem. There is no indication that Stevens went onto the New Jersey side, so he must have crossed the Hudson. If he did, an overall walking speed at five miles per hour would increase the overall duration of the trip by one hour. (An average walking speed of three miles per hour would result in a minimum of fourteen or more hours.) That means by 7am he'd still have 39 miles to go. While Stevens indicates walking with minimal rest, his journey requires five miles per hour — this would take approximately nine hours in the most generous approximation. Is that possible? For one, he had engaged nature and made several observations and sketches in his notebook. Moreover, the terrain was not entirely flat. Nonetheless, he claims to end walking by 6:30pm, thus nine hours, then caught a train back. The subway would not be active until September of that year, although there was active train service. He notes "I thought, on the train, how utterly we have forsaken the Earth, in the sense of excluding it from our thoughts."[8] Perhaps he was still appraising Organismus? What seems clear is a renewed reverence for the Earth, which is a common feature of experiencer testimony whereby apocalyptic scenes are presented by their captors. Had Stevens a similar experience? Were principled ideas about planetary preservation installed? Earth reverence is sustained in the oeuvre again and again, notably in 1948, regarding the "poem of the earth" which "remains to be written."[9] Conversely, indications that missing time occurred

---

7   Stevens, *Letters of Wallace Stevens,* 71 (no. 89).
8   Ibid., 73 (no. 89).
9   Stevens, *Collected Poetry and Prose,* 730. John Mack's summation is illustrative: "Indeed, it seems to me quite possible that the protection of the Earth's life is at the heart of the abduction phenomenon. Astonishingly, the damage we have been inflicting upon the Earth's life-forms appears not to have gone 'unnoticed' by whatever intelligence or creative principle dwells in the cosmos, and it is providing some sort of feedback to us, however

on this hike are difficult to determine. For example, "From the Palisades, I looked down on the Hudson, which glimmered incessantly. In the distance, the Sound shot up a flare. There was a ship below me + I made note of the whole business in a sketch on a scrap of paper, which I copy. Will it help me remember the thing."[10] He soon notes "I heard a dry murmur in the reeds (may I never forget it)" then remarks the ship sketched were the "Mary Ann."[11] I think it's a stretch to claim this were staging—however, the poem and the beam stay with me. The journal was a recollection after all. Beyond his reading habits, I need ask where this poem comes from, exactly? He's almost done with law school and the life of letters is somewhat behind him. It may well be a bit of decompression in the end.

If we don't have enough evidence to confidently determine contact occurred on April 18, 1904, consider an entry from December 31, 1900, months prior to the Central Park owl experience from the previous chapter:

> Quarter-of-twelve. The noise is rather confused + sounds like a horse-fly buzzing around the room. Ferries are tooting + chimes have broken out.
>
> Horrid din — The Hour strikes — like roar of heavy express — or rolling of great mill — Chimes incoherent, Voices — Mass of sound-like strong wind through telegraph wires. January 1 — 1901 — Bon Jour.
>
> Noise still great — noise within noise — noise — noise — noise — but it seems to be subsiding.
>
> I was trying to say a prayer but could not.[12]

---

strange its form appears to be." John E. Mack, "Chapter 5: Protecting the Earth," in *Passport to the Cosmos* (White Crow Books, 1999), 94–119.

10 Stevens, *Letters of Wallace Stevens*, 71–72 (no. 89).

11 Ibid., 72 (no. 89).

12 Ibid., 49–50 (no. 54).

If the noises that the young Stevens hears are merely those of New Year's Eve revelry, it would not negate abduction before or simply on that day. Yet it is utterly bizarre to think he were. Humming sounds often appear in Stevens's verse. In late 1900, what could have caused this sound? Electricity had been supplied for a few years to the Greenwich Village area of Manhattan, where Stevens resided, more precisely on 37 West 9th Street. Thomas Edison's Pearl Street Station was likely the grid source. Early electric generators created a humming sound (and they were noisy, as were the cables which carried electricity). However, it's unlikely Stevens was close enough to hear them, as the Pearl Street Station was about two miles from his apartment. Moreover, the reference to wind through telegraph wires "sound-like" which is a comparison but not necessarily the source. An idle mind may expand everyday sounds into something engorged. In other words, maybe he interpreted sounds in the playground of expanding perception. Perhaps his desire for spiritual reconnection resulted in encounters with NHI, as he was in a meditative posture attempting to pray?

John Mack's *Abductions* remarks on a regressee named Scott whose experiences may be analogous to Stevens's:

> His abduction experiences [...] had made clear to him that "there's a massive amount of information in my head that I can't even understand." The aliens, he suggested, are "helping us grow so we can comprehend them... They're getting us trained to get us to a point where we can deal with them."[13]

Stevens's entry from April 18, 1904, remains impressive in this regard. What to make of his complete astonishment with the color blue which "seems as if it were the dusk of the lost Pleiades, as if it were a twilight where any moment the fairies might light their lamps"?[14] Blue, as observed, has a prominent role in

---

13 John E. Mack, *Abduction: Human Encounters with Aliens* (Scribner, 1994), 99.
14 Stevens, *Letters of Wallace Stevens*, 72 (no. 89).

terms of shadows and the curious, ambiguously gendered presence pervading the verse, specifically found in "Dolls," "Yellow Afternoon," and "The Well-Dressed Man with a Beard."

A skeptical challenge to Stevens's fairy seeking and an obsession with blue, particular to September 4, 1902 and April 18, 1904 could point to Tomkins Quarry, which began operation in the late 1850s. The quarry is approximately one mile south of Tomkins Cove. Inactive quarries fill up with water and obtain hues of blue due to their mineralized content. Key to this argument is whether or not the site was active in 1904. If active, constant water drainage would be required to maintain operations. At least one image found shows it dry, empty, and active in 1890.[15] Other images from 1910[16] and 1912[17] show activity and insignificant pooling. Officially the quarry shut down in 2012 which allowed it to fill up.[18] We will likely never know the state of operations when Stevens visited the area. And one may only speculate about alien life form procuring minerals from the earth from such sites. Then there is the Hudson River — yet to my knowledge rivers are not blue, especially in the spring. We cannot exclude Long Island Sound but without knowing the precise vantage point it is difficult to ascertain. What about the sky, a primary feature of his early journals? What to make of the "lost Pleiades" which concerns "Faith, that point about the fairies is only too true." To whom does he refer to, if not himself? What to make of the poem which metaphorically situates the Pleiadean constellation with a vine of Columbine blooms?:

---

15 "Tomkins Cove quarry, Stony Point, NY," *New York Heritage Digital Collections*, 1890, https://cdm16694.contentdm.oclc.org/digital/collection/nyacklib/id/3815.

16 "Tomkins Cove quarry," *New York Heritage Digital Collections*, 1910, https://cdm16694.contentdm.oclc.org/digital/collection/larc/id/2536/rec/28.

17 "Stone Quarry, Tomkins Cove, N.Y.," *New York Heritage Digital Collections*, 1912, https://cdm16694.contentdm.oclc.org/digital/collection/larc/id/2531.

18 Rock Products News, "Former New York Quarry May Get New Life," *Rock Products*, March 28, 2019, https://rockproducts.com/2019/03/28/former-new-york-quarry-may-get-new-life/.

"I would pursue / The beam that brings / So sweet a hope / Of sweeter things."[19] What is this beam?

Regarding abduction scholarship, consistencies appear when compared to Stevens's entries from December 31, 1900 and April 18, 1904. Abduction or contact encounters begin in homes or while operating cars. Writes Mack: "In some cases the experiencer may be walking in nature. One woman reported being taken from a snowmobile on a winter's day." Children have been taken from school yards as well:

> The first indication that an abduction is about to occur might be an unexplained intense blue or white light that floods the bedroom, an odd buzzing or humming sound, unexplained apprehension, the sense of an unusual presence or even the direct sighting of one or more humanoid beings in the room, and, of course, the close-up sighting of a strange craft.[20]

Throughout the poems, blue and white are a common feature. There are occasions of buzzing and humming, incoherent speaking or telepathic implications of dialogue: recall "dialogues between incognitos" and those "voluble shadows." In "The Irrational Element in Poetry," a strange recollection of a waking state intimates a possible connection. There Stevens recalls that, upon the snow a thin layer of ice had formed outside his window. Under a nearly full moon, recalls Stevens:

> I awoke once several hours before daylight and as I lay in bed I heard the steps of a cat running over the snow under my window almost inaudibly. The faintness and strangeness of the sound made on me one of those impressions which one so often seizes as pretexts for poetry.[21]

---

19 Stevens, *Collected Poetry and Prose,* 513–14.
20 Mack, *Abduction: Human Encounters with Aliens,* 35–36.
21 Stevens, *Collected Poetry and Prose,* 782.

Once more, the dream state comes into play. How to know it was a cat beneath the window when lying in bed? Moreover, cats are strewn throughout the oeuvre. In *The Man with the Blue Guitar* we have a reprise on "deep, voluble shadows" as "liquid cats / Moved in the grass without a sound."[22] What follows is perhaps more bizarre. Of his dream state recollection, Stevens opines something strange:

> Poets continue to be born not made and cannot, I am afraid, be predetermined. While, on the one hand, if they could be predetermined, they might long since have become extinct, they might, on the other hand, have changed life from what it is today into one of those transformations in which they delight, and they might have seen to it that they greatly multiplied themselves there.[23]

The primary idea is the transformation of humanity by way of poets. This concerns extinction or multiplication of a species. It is hard to understand Stevens's point of view as if it were not necessarily human. For comparison, consider the following from Mack:

> When an abduction begins during the night, or, as is common, during the early hours of the morning, the experiencer may at first call what is happening a dream. But careful questioning will reveal that the experiencer had not fallen asleep at all, or that the experience began in a conscious state after awakening. As the abduction begins the abductee may experience a subtle shift of consciousness, but this state of being is just as real, or even more so, than the "normal" one.[24]

---

22 Ibid., 146.

23 Ibid., 782.

24 "Sometimes there is a moment of shock and sadness when the abductee discovers in the initial interview, or during a hypnosis session, that what they had more comfortably held to be a dream was actually some sort of bizarre, threatening, and vivid experience which they may then recall

What is observed here is a dream state and a curious, undefined presence in Mack's abductee and Stevens's account of a cat, as well as the sense of extra- or nonhuman functionality or commutation as a result.

"A Dream, to Call It a Dream"

In a 1993 panel discussion, John Mack rhetorically asks his audience a question: "what is a dream to an abductee?"[25] Through hypnotic regression he found something of a normative truth; that the moment contact begins is precisely when one believes one is asleep. Suppose the shift in consciousness, not sleep, to be the case; that during hypnosis one realizes one was actually awake — not asleep — thus in a theta state of consciousness. Noting the limits of the English language, Mack excitedly remarked, "We do not have language for that."[26] But perhaps we do? For the passage between mortals and the unnamed, the saying of the unsaid, is learned to us through the experience of strong poets. Whether this concerns metalogic or metalanguage, at base it begs the absolute. That what we call absolute refers to a real, an exterior, which certain poets have expressed quite well. Of this exterior would we find the domain of other beings and what is otherwise incommensurable. And within this irrational element, they watch into our time and venture into it, from without. Such irrationality cannot be appropriated if we continue with the impoverishing of language as it is. By this I do not mean the incommensurability of global languages. I mean language in relation to mind over, against, and through the grammar of globalizing technologies. Prompt bots train us to flatten the mind. We forfeit depth for the ease of interpretation. Yet to

---

has occurred repeatedly and for which they have no explanation." Mack, *Abduction*, 35.

25 Eyes on Cinema, "Abductees and Researchers Talk About the Alien Abduction Phenomenon, April 1993," *YouTube*, September 2, 2022, https://www.youtube.com/watch?v=Gw4o-Qd4jlA. John Mack's comments are at 1:30:00.

26 Ibid.

THE BLUE GODS OF ORGANISMUS

develop commensurability requires precisely what evades us in an ever-increasing, globally intelligent, "smart" world.

As for dreams, let us first consider poem XVIII of "The Man with the Blue Guitar" (1937) where I believe the object faced regards what Stevens meant by an "absolute object."[27] For that I ask what this absolute object could represent in the oeuvre if not the UFO? And yet the UFO, whether a self-generated, Jungian mandala or extra-terrestrial/tempestral NHI, suggests that the poem — through its special purchase on language as code — is a human-specific technology that captures commutation with NHI. That is, poems are the residuum of an intelligent mandala and for that a technology that offers unique insight to mind, if not "source." Thus of the absolute object we turn to the poem:

A dream (to call it a dream) in which
I can believe, in face of the object,

A dream no longer a dream, a thing,
Of things as they are, as the blue guitar

After long strumming on certain nights
Gives the touch of the senses, not of the hand,

But the very senses as they touch
The wind-gloss. Or as daylight comes,

---

27 "Absolute object" was a primary subject of my doctoral dissertation on Stevens. This term was almost certainly adopted from the French philosopher and poet he befriends, Jean André Wahl (1888–1974) and his book *The Philosopher's Way* (1948). Stevens had written to Barabara Church on June 22, 1948, remarking that he was reading Wahl's book. Stevens, *Letters of Wallace Stevens*, 601 (no. 655). Absolute object appears in "From the Notebooks" with the date "1948?" in Stevens, *Collected Poetry and Prose*, 921. Wahl references this "absolute object" with regard to Søren Kierkegaard. Jean Wahl, *The Philosophers Way* (Oxford University Press, 1948), 283–84. See Adam Staley Groves, "The Poetic Subject: A Theory of Poetry According to the Poet Wallace Stevens and the Philosopher Jean Wahl" (PhD diss., University of Aberdeen, 2016).

> Like light in a mirroring of cliffs,
> Rising upward from a sea of ex.[28]

Rising from a sea of nothing is the object. And the sea is the night on which thinking stirs, where the intelligence pushes upward, embossing incessantly, as if the veil of a breathing doll, as if the doll were breathing from the unconscious into reflection. By thinking not thought we find that churning exterior of language, an unrecognized logic; contours of an alien form. The object is observed, but only as pieces or facets, a type of *rifacimento* upon the cliffs and not whole. The object repairs or constructs in the plurality of the possible (within the finitude of human signification).

Dramatically the dream is not a dream until we name it. As with hypnotic regression, the experiencer reappropriates aspects of consciousness that a productive body captured, previously spirited away by intelligent deception. Yet the poem reclaims the dream of an encounter. Enters then an affirmation of belief as the *object* becomes a *thing* when *facing* it. We name it, it's ours, and as with poetry, the answer and the title most often come first. Recall a similar repatriation of consciousness from "Owl's Clover": "The portent may itself be memory; / And memory may itself be time to come / And must be, when the portent, changed, takes on / A mask up-gathered brilliantly from the dirt."[29]

Poem XIX of "The Man with the Blue Guitar" questions the monster reduced to the self that "in face of the monster" one would "be more than part / Of it, more than the monstrous player of":

> One of its monstrous lutes, not be
> Alone, but reduce the monster and be,
>
> Two things, the two together as one,

---

28 Stevens, *Collected Poetry and Prose*, 143.
29 Ibid., 169.

> And play of the monster and of myself,
>
> Or better not of myself at all,
> But of that as its intelligence,
>
> Being the lion in the lute
> Before the lion locked in stone.[30]

Is it not obvious "as its intelligence" is something won? What follows is an overcoming of the monster/self dyad in poem XX, which questions what's "in life except one's ideas," a question directed to "Good air, good friend, what is there in life?" This seems an outpouring of the heart: "Good air, my only friend, believe," which "would be a brother full / Of love, believe would be a friend, // Friendlier than my only friend, / Good air."[31] Poem XXI initiates a maxim:

> A substitute for all the gods:
> This self, not that gold self aloft,
>
> Alone, one's shadow magnified,
> Lord of the body, looking down,
>
> As now and called most high,
> The shadow of Chocorua
>
> In an immenser heaven, aloft,
> Alone, lord of the land and lord
>
> Of the men that live in the land, high lord.
> One's self and the mountains of one's land,

---

30 Ibid., 143.
31 Ibid., 144.

Without shadows, without magnificence,
The flesh, the bone, the dirt, the stone.[32]

"The Man with the Blue Guitar" was composed in the mid-1930s. Recall "Chocorua to Its Neighbor" originates in the early 1940s, but here is a recollection years before. Recall: "Now, I, Chocorua, speak of this shadow as / A human thing. It is an eminence."[33] Elanor Cook does not elaborate in the same direction, noting that it only occurs in both poems regarding shadow. Moreover, she claims this is "a search for belief" but that the imagination has failed.[34] While the solitary is evident, as is the struggle of belief, for me this replays the desire of voluble shadows, a loneliness that desires commutation with an intelligence, brother, and friend as with "Chocorua to Its Neighbor." Contrary to Cook, the imagination does not fail in the mode of metaphysics. For Stevens the unreal comes from a real and it is our situatedness with the illusion termed reality that we must confront. In other words, imagination is a means by which disclosure occurs to the individual through poetry. Consider poem XIX above: "Or better not of myself at all, / But of that as its intelligence," as an acceptance of agency. How else to say it? How else to understand the role of Chocorua? By poem XXII we find a link to missing time and "the absence in reality" for which the poem stores and discloses. Here the primary role of the poem is defined:

Poetry is the subject of the poem,
From this the poem issues and

To this returns. Between the two,
Between issue and return, there is

---

32 Ibid.
33 Ibid., 267.
34 Elanor Cook, *Reader's Guide to Wallace Stevens* (Princeton University Press, 2007), 124.

An absence in reality,
Things as they are. Or so we say.

But are these separate? Is it
An absence for the poem, which acquires

Its true appearances there, sun's green,
Cloud's red, earth feeling, sky that thinks?

From these it takes. Perhaps it gives,
In the universal intercourse.[35]

Poetry presents the proof of an intelligent other which its technology appropriates. If one may create their own UFO, it is equally a commutation at the level of metalogic from a real. After all, what Stevens expounds in his theory of the 1930s was an attempt to explain why he writes poetry, has "poetic sensibility," and he applies this form to poems through a relational capability termed "poetic mechanism." This attempt to rationalize NHI experience leads him to distinguish born poets from made poets, that is, I suppose with caution, engineered forms of life who would multiply themselves "there" or would otherwise extinct themselves with an unbridled, mental power.

"Disclosure […] certainly to myself"

If poetry's role in the disclosure of NHI, in my mind, is evident, could Stevens's "monster" in the 1930s refer to an alien-self, something not human or more human? Moreover, is it the disclosure of such which augments thinking into knowledge, as a knowing we are capable of attaining? Stevens seems to suggest this in "The Irrational Element in Poetry" which declares:

> if the irrational element is merely poetic energy, it is to be found wherever poetry is to be found. One such manifes-

---

35 Stevens, *Collected Poetry and Prose*, 145.

tation is the disclosure of the individuality of the poet. It is unlikely that this disclosure is ever visible as plainly to anyone as to the poet himself.[36]

By "wherever poetry is to be found" are we to think wherever NHI occurs? This would regard "Owl's Clover" and the statue as variable symbol, says Stevens:

> I wanted to deal with exactly such a subject and I chose that as a bit of reality, actuality, the contemporaneous. But I wanted the result to be poetry so far as I was able to write poetry. To be specific, I wanted to apply my own sensibility to something perfectly matter-of-fact. The result would be a disclosure of my own sensibility or individuality, as I called it a moment ago, certainly to myself.[37]

Does the statue spark a trigger moment ushering in a recollection of early 1901 and the Angel of the Waters fountain? Was it subsequently applied to a poem composed thirty years later? If a trigger of involuntary memory perhaps this statement was a matter of coping; that Stevens claims to intentionally trigger in the now, as it were. What we do know is that Stevens is aware of strange encounters which breach ordinary self-conception. Compare this to what comes in 1943, by way of introducing the work of a new poet, Samuel French Morse:

> As the writer of such poems becomes more and more the master of his own poetry: that is to say, as he becomes better able to realize his individual perceptions, and as he acquires faith in his function as poet, he is likely to project the rigors of his early work into what he does later. So that his early work really discloses his identity.[38]

---

36 Ibid., 783.
37 Ibid., 783–84.
38 Stevens, *Collected Poetry and Prose*, 811.

Both born and made poets face a predetermination. By poetry we have a capacity to self-disclose and overcome the deception of our reality. We are compelled by something exquisitely abstract thus are able to change it. What Stevens reveals is the enlargement of reality by way of the mind. Poem and poet augur a novel conscious substance which current knowledge finds unreal if not alien. For Stevens it comes to an "instinctive […] will to believe."[39] If such will, as instinct, characterizes his cosmic augmentation, this seems more apparent by 1942 regarding a poet's feeling when writing, when one finds a level of saintliness:

> The feeling is not a feeling peculiar to exquisite or (perhaps, as better) precise realization, and hence confined to poets who exceed us in nature as they do in speech. There is nothing rare about it although it may extend to degrees of rarity. On the contrary, just as [philosopher Henri] Bergson refers to the simpler representations of aspiration occurring in the lives of the saints, so we may refer to the simpler representations of an aspiration (not the same, yet not wholly unlike) occurring in the lives of those who have just written their first essential poems. After all, the young man or young woman who has written a few poems and who wants to read them is merely the *voluble convert* or the person looking in a mirror who sees suddenly the traces of an *unexpected genealogy*. We are interested in this transformation primarily on the part of the poet. Yet it is a thing that communicates itself to the reader. Anyone who has read a long poem day after day as, for example, *The Faerie Queene,* knows how the poem comes to possess the reader and how it naturalizes him in its own imagination and liberates him there.[40]

---

[39] Stevens, *Letters of Wallace Stevens,* 430 (no. 467).
[40] Stevens, *Collected Poetry and Prose,* 673. My emphasis.

The dream is, as with Mack, a steady congruence, a "subtle shift of consciousness."[41] Clearly Stevens experiences this shift with the Central Park owl of 1901, the owl of 1902, and during his 1904 adventure to Tomkins Cove. In other words, the first essential poems come to reveal genealogic mirroring, the confrontation with an alien-self through the content of literature and lived experience. If we parse the contemporary abductee story — that one is at first terrorized by being taken captive (we have no terror in Stevens's journals, moreover some abductees report no terror at all) — we may suppose a commutative acceptance or what Mack calls "the alien self," his observation of a "peculiar sense that many abductees […] have a dual human/alien identity […] For the alien self is felt to be a kind of missing part, a soul link to the universal source of consciousness, the anima mundi from which they feel they have been cut off."[42] In that way, when we face the absolute object, we initiate a reconnection to base reality and subsequently must deal with reality as metaphysics.

That NHI are masterful intelligences situating their commutation with humans through literature is not an exotic claim. Anyone who has bothered to study hermeneutics understands what happens in translation. Of course, we are not focusing on the technical-interpretive dimension rather the understanding between 'beings' as poetic relation, the irreducible field between two things which marks the limit of empirical sense-perception according to materialist doctrine. It is not hard to see congruency between Stevens's journals and verse with what Mack reports. Specifically, the translation between alien and self;

---

41 "As the abduction begins the abductee may experience a subtle shift of consciousness, but this state of being is just as real, or even more so, than the "normal" one. Sometimes there is a moment of shock and sadness when the abductee discovers in the initial interview, or during a hypnosis session, that what they had more comfortably held to be a dream was actually some sort of bizarre, threatening, and vivid experience which they may then recall has occurred repeatedly and for which they have no explanation." Mack, *Abduction*, 35.

42 Ibid., 413.

inhuman and human. Recalling Stevens's later thoughts about "Supreme Fiction" and "whether or not, it must be human", the issue gains in intrigue. Such ideation can be found in many instances of verse, for example, "Angel Surrounded by Paysans", from which an angel announces, "I am the angel of reality. / Seen for a moment standing at the door." This gives way to questioning the artificiality of one's human existence, echoing the monster of "The Man with the Blue Guitar" reprised in "Angel Surrounded by Paysans":

> Am I not
> Myself, only half a figure of a sort,
>
> A figure half seen, or seen for a moment, a man
> Of the mind, an apparition apparelled in
>
> Apparels of such lightest look that a turn
> Of my shoulder and quickly, too quickly, I am gone?[43]

Ye Sounde

Tomkins Cove, where I suppose Stevens has another NHI experience on April 18, 1904, was determined a UFO hotspot in the 1970s.[44] This encounter took place at Stony Point on the Hudson River, the same place of a major UFO sighting in 1984.[45] Revealed is the potential for a pattern of encounters beyond Stevens's words, as reported by *The New York Times* in 1976.[46] What then

---

43 Stevens, *Collected Poetry and Prose,* 423.
44 As with Stevens's accounts of Mt. Chocorua and the Betty and Barney Hill case of 1961.
45 The documentation of encounters, contact, and abductions as well as photographic evidence associated with the "1984 Hudson Valley UFO sightings" is compelling. See Saving VHS Tapes, "The Hudson Valley UFO Sightings Dr. J. Allen Hynek, Phillip J. Imbrogo — Close Encounters of the 4th Kind," *YouTube,* November, 27, 2020, https://www.youtube.com/watch?v=2fQgrYLUfjo.
46 "Rockland U.F.O. 'Invasion' Starts Round of Explanations," *The New York Times,* October 11, 1976, https://www.nytimes.com/1976/10/11/archives/

to make of the "lost Pleidians" Stevens refers to in 1904, considering his sense of urgency regarding humans who have "utterly forsaken the Earth?":

> Man is an affair of cities. His gardens + orchards + fields are mere scrapings. Somehow, however, he has managed to shut out the face of the giant from his windows. But the giant is there, nevertheless. And it is a proper question, whether or not the Lilliputians have tied him down. There are his huge legs, Africa + South America, still, apparently, free; and the rest of him is pretty tough and unhandy. But, as I say, we do not think of this. There was a girl on the train with a face like the under-side of a moonfish. Her talk was of dances + men. For her, Sahara had no sand; Brazil, no mud.[47]

Some experiencers describe alien visages to have the skin quality of a dolphin. Even if I do not want to lean too much on the moonfish analogy, it is nonetheless perturbing. Was our poet followed home? References to a woman made of wax in "Infernale" suggest that this figure is further transformed as a subject of the poem. Following this is a suggestion ora meditation on reincarnation. From the *Uncollected Poems* (approx. 1913–1914) says "Infernale":

> *(A boor of night in middle earth cries out.)*
> Hola! Hola! What steps are those that break
> This crust of air?… (*He pauses.*) Can breath shake
> The solid wax from which the warmth dies out?…
>
> I saw a waxen woman in a smock
> Fly from the black toward the purple air.
> (*He shouts.*) Hola! Of that strange light, beware!
> (*A woman's voice is heard, replying.*) Mock

---

rockland-ufo-invasion-starts-round-of-explanations.html.
47 Stevens, *Letters of Wallace Stevens*, 73 (no. 89).

The bondage of the Stygian concubine,
Hallooing haggler; for the wax is blown,
And downward, from this purple region, thrown;
And I fly forth, the naked Proserpine.

(Her pale smock sparkles in a light begun
To be diffused, and, as she disappears,
The silent watcher, far below her, hears;)
Soaring Olympus glitters in the sun.[48]

"Infernale" presents a confoundment. First, there are steps to Olympus, which "glitters in the sun," a similar feature of the later "Pieces." Note that the mythological home of the Greek gods is soaring—as if a craft. Then that "strange light" and the flying Persephone (Romanized Proserpine) moving from the river Styx; a bound concubine breaking free. The conflation of mythological figures is hard to parse, and the imprint of literature bears heavily, namely Spencer's *Faerie Queene*. Conversely, if we read the italicized portions of "Infernale" they feel more testimonial, as with the journal entry which we began this chapter:

From the boor of night in middle earth cries out.
He pauses.

He shouts.
A woman's voice is heard, replying.

Her pale smock sparkles in a light begun
To be diffused, and, as she disappears,
The silent watcher, far below her, hears;

By isolating the italicized phrases do we find that moonfish-belly-faced woman on the train? As for the "boor of night," some crude, voluble shadow-creature? Is it something within the earth that emerges; shoots into the air? Recall: "to space?"

---

48 Stevens, *Collected Poetry and Prose*, 518.

Her form dissolves while he watches from beneath. Again, there is breath, but this time "And I fly forth." There is a dialogue but of a "silent watcher." It seems nonsensical but intentional. An untitled poem that follows "Infernale" is more direct:

> All things imagined are of earth compact,
> Strange beast and bird, strange creatures all;
> Strange minds of men, unwilling slaves to fact:
>
> Struggling with desperate clouds, they still proclaim
> The rushing pearl, the whirling black,
> Clearly, in well-remembered word and name.
>
> Even the dead, when they return, return
> Not as those dead, concealed away;
> But their old persons move again, and burn.[49]

Beyond the extraterrestrial hypothesis we have openings to interdimensional theory. In *Passport to Magonia,* Jacques Vallee formulates an early iteration:

> The physical nature of Magonia [...] is a remote country, an invisible island, some faraway place one can reach only by a long journey. Indeed, in some tales, it is a celestial country [...]. This parallels the belief in the extraterrestrial origin of UFOs [...]. A second — and equally widespread — theory, is that Elfland constitutes a sort of parallel universe, which coexists with our own. It is made visible and tangible only to selected people, and the "doors" that lead through it are tangential points, known only to the elves.[50]

For Stevens, door swings between dimensions wherefrom "All things imagined are of earth compact," that is, "strange creatures all," concern a circuitry of the earth-poem. Recall that in poem

---

49 Ibid.
50 Vallee, *Passport to Magonia,* 141.

XXII of "The Man with the Blue Guitar" we find the same conceptual passage that "Poetry is the subject of the poem / from this issues and / To this returns. [...] Between [...], there is / An absence in reality,"[51] that in the poem there are "true appearances" which "Infernale" italicizes twenty years prior. Such absences in reality may well be missing time as with the poems studied in the Chapter One.

Thirty years before, the color blue, as with the man with the blue guitar, concerns one who plays a lyre as had "One of the fairies singing to his harp."[52] Perhaps blue is a code originating from the 1900s? As to the journal entry of April 18, 1904, Stevens had mentioned the Pleiades, which in UFO lore are supposedly home to "Nordic Aliens." These "space brothers" are supposedly giants concerned with the Earth's health, and initiate contact with human beings. Did Stevens have contact? Or was he simply an avid reader who lived deep in his imagination? Could it be both? Two footnotes appended to this entry state the following:

> The sketch is in the journal with "ye sounde" written beside it.

> The map in the Journal is accompanied by the following: *"Notes on ye above Mappe of ye Hudson R.* At this point, ye distance was as blue as the eyes of a Norsk virgin. + Here lies Stony Point, where ye battle was fought. A damned queer place for a battle.[53]

What then of the "Lilliputians" or little men who have yet to tie down the giant: is this not a scene from *Gulliver's Travels*, Jonathan Swift's "traveler's tale," which first appeared in 1726? Was Stevens tied down, restrained on the table surrounded by little dolls or dwarves? What to make of this giant who man has managed to shut out from view at the expense of the Earth? Is it

---

51 Stevens, *Collected Poetry and Prose*, 144–45.
52 Stevens, *Letters of Wallace Stevens*, 72 (no. 89).
53 Ibid., 72n2, n3.

a reflection of apocalyptic scenes, force fed, as it were? Readers will likely know the giant's role in Stevens's oeuvre. For example, "Presence of an External Master of Knowledge"[54]; poem VIII of "Things of August"[55]; and, more curiously, the early poem "The Plot against the Giant," which is more erotic, recalls the ear Stevens remarks of in the April 18, 1901 entry.

Did Stevens read Swift? At Harvard, Letters reveals Stevens read *The Death of Swift* as late as 1899 receiving high marks.[56] Moreover, *Gulliver's Travels* is one of several fictive works that feature the flying island "Laputa." The literary element expressed by Stevens's NHI encounters has congruency with Vallee's interdimensional thesis, that UFOs are most likely not explicit spacecraft, and that "the extraterrestrial theory is not strange enough to explain the facts." In other words, "the UFO phenomenon represents evidence for other dimensions beyond spacetime." Thus, if there is "a system around us that transcends time as it transcends space," it would mean a mastery that "may well be able to locate itself in outer space." However, "its manifestations cannot be spacecraft in the ordinary nuts and bolts sense." As echoed by Mike Clelland, Vallee is consistent in his belief that physical manifestations of NHI "cannot be understood apart from their psychic and symbolic reality" for it is "a spiritual system that acts on and uses humans."[57] The influence of NHI in literature may be transmedial, such forms transposing between subject and object by way of poetic mechanisms that are otherwise articulations of one's own mandala. Speculating broadly, a transmediality would mean a capacity of literature or poetic technology to facilitate a convening with NHI.

---

54 Stevens, *Collected Poetry and Prose*, 467.
55 Ibid., 421.
56 Stevens, *Letters of Wallace Stevens*, 23 (no. 21). In 1940, Stevens also refers to the author in a letter to critic Hi Simons. Ibid., 347 (no. 396).
57 Jacques Vallee, *Alien Contact Trilogy*, vol. 1: *Dimensions: A Casebook of Alien Contact* (Anomalist Books, 2003), 283–85.

Blue about Blue

The self-generated UFO, Jung's mandala, is a poetic creation, a protopoem between dimensions wherefrom the expansion of reality is something "in which I can believe."[58] If so, let us take a ride. "Landscape with Boat" implies the encounters of Central Park from February 7, 1901 and with more certainty Tomkins Cove on April 18, 1904. A revision of the journaled poem from April 18 may have occurred in "The Little June Book," circa April 1909. Things get weirder considering the note "ye sounde," or, more precisely, the figure of the ear across the oeuvre. The ear detects the mode of commutation with the comedian, the primitive, or the ancients.[59]

"Landscape with Boat" begins this way: "An anti-masterman, floribund ascetic" and progresses to the experience of floating naked in the air. It confronts "the colossal illusion of heaven" and blue is the object of many lines:

> He wanted the eye to see
> And not be touched by blue. He wanted to know,
> A naked man who regarded himself in the glass
> Of Air, who looked for the world beneath the blue,
> Without blue, without any turquoise tint or phase.[60]

The truth becomes a matter of confusion, a matter which can be found in Adagia: "The loss of language creates confusion or dumbness."[61]

> It was nowhere else, its place had to be supposed,
> Itself had to be supposed, a thing supposed
> In a place supposed, a thing that he reached
> In a place that he reached, by rejecting what he saw

---

58 Stevens, *Collected Poetry and Prose*, 143.
59 "He will bend his ear then." Ibid., 6.
60 Ibid., 220.
61 Ibid., 901.

> And denying what he heard. He would arrive.
> He had only not to live, to walk in the dark,
> To be projected by one void into
> Another.
>
> It was his nature to suppose,
> To receive what others had supposed, without
> Accepting. He received what he denied.
> But as truth to be accepted, he supposed
> A truth beyond all truths[62]

This reads as both acceptance and a coming to terms:

> He never supposed divine
> Things might not look divine, nor that if nothing
> Was divine then all things were, the world itself,
> And that if nothing was the truth, then all
> Things were the truth, the world itself was the truth.[63]

How to consider an alien-self if not by the lines which precede it?:

> He never supposed
> That he might be truth, himself, or part of it,
> That the things he rejected might be part
> And the irregular turquoise, part, the perceptible blue
> Grown denser, part, the so touched, so played
> Upon the clouds, the ear so magnified.[64]

If here we find sadness or consternation it is equally remorse if not regret, and it hurts:

---

62 Ibid., 220–21.
63 Ibid., 221.
64 Ibid., 220–21.

> Had he been better able to suppose:
> He might sit on a sofa on a balcony
> Above the Mediterranean, emerald
> Becoming emeralds. He might watch the palms
> Flap green ears in the heat. He might observe
> A yellow wine and follow a steamer's track
> And say, "The thing I hum appears to be
> The rhythm of this celestial pantomime."[65]

Once more humming and its cosmic composition. This poem carries the signature of April 18, 1904 and reconstitutes the experience with a tonality different from much of his verse. How does one deny the poem and the owl which follows, titled "On the Adequacy of Landscape"? If this is experiencer testimony, it is Stevens's solitary acceptance. What then is left if not some tepid academical conclusion? That poetry and prose were attempts to heal yet equally embolden estrangement? Let us assume he tried the best he could within the framework of his own ego and time. That becoming a famous poet a few years earlier delivered more emptiness. That fame was deceptive, a hope to be heard. Stevens didn't need the money. For all the critical accounts of Stevens's aloofness and questions of character, one should consider him again. Stevens reveals NHI experiences in his early journals. We can see his loquacious talent and lifelong eagerness to understand philosophy helped him render experiences in verse and theorize them. Yet by the time his fame was established, he may well have guarded his experiences more closely. So goes "ye sounde." So goes the work of a mortal poet and the color yellow.

---

65 Ibid., 221.

5

Xretism

> I wondered when they would get in touch with me again and
> how? Had they meant soon—or would it be months or even
> years? These and hundreds of similar questions clamored in my
> mind. I wondered if I was under constant observation by them.
> If so, I thought that through telepathy I could signal them to
> return. One night I went back to that lonely spot on Forest
> Lawn Drive and tried to establish telepathic communication.
> But it was useless! No glowing red disk appeared—only the
> night and the empty skies that gave back no answer.
> — Orfeo Angelucci[1]

The phenomenon is characteristically absurd. One example is parallels between Stevens's early years and a somewhat dubious book *The Shocking Truth*. Written by Albert Coe, it concerns the years 1901–1904 and depictions of an alien he claims to encountered in the 1920s. Stevens's Tompkins Cove experience of April 18, 1904, and the Central Park owl experience of 1901 as well as the owl of 1902 fit this timeframe. Coe claims to have remained in contact with this alien until the 1970s, in person and through

---

1 Orfeo M. Angelucci, *The Secret of the Saucers* (Amherst Press, 1955), 18–19.

letters.[2] Weirdly, there are indications of a similar friend in Stevens's verse. According to Coe in 1901, this alien recalled a gathering of "colleagues [...] in a conference hall, to discuss an issue of vital importance with their governing council, an eminent body comprising twenty-eight men and twenty-eight women, each an elected representative of the fifty-six sciences. The topic of concentrated interest was this same earth and its modern inhabitant." At issue was the "development of advanced technologies" and "with each new discovery; new invention, every war was becoming a little more deadly." The beings devised a plan of "intimate contact with the people of Earth, through a cryptic infiltration" in order to "[s]tudy with them, work with them, as one of their own" so that "[a]ny spectacular breakthrough could then be immediately evaluated." From 1901 forward contact was "accomplished in two years and the one hundred 'volunteers' carrier to the designated cities of every major country on Earth, during the months from February to June of 1904 in an unprecedented method, to infiltrate a nucleus, that may anticipate and forestall any future debacle resulting from the misdirected genious of the human brain."

Coe claims that the aliens had several honor-bound codes of conduct. Contact secrecy was "paramount" and intervention or change in human affairs "was strictly prohibited." These beings could not participate in warfare or "divulge any secret" regarding sciences which would aid military conflict. No human could enter a space craft and male aliens could have relations with human females though they were to conduct themselves "as gentlemen," if only to contribute to an earth inhabitant's happiness.[3] If there are congruencies with Stevens's accounts, it would be desire for actual contact. Stevens's flight in several poems such as "Landscape with Boat" diverges a bit. However, in "Dolls" the poet thinks he is interacting with a female being only

---

[2] Coe did not reveal the story to his wife or anyone else until the book was published. The citations that follow are from Albert Coe, *The Shocking Truth* (1969), 87–90.

[3] Ibid., 89–90.

to remark of "Another" by questioning if he was being tricked by "greybeards."[4] Writes Coe: "In the beginning quite a controversy developed with the female element, through their desire to volunteer for this worthy mission; but after explanation and decision, by the council, they were convinced of the impracticability of exposure to the unfamiliar and barbaric practices of Earth."[5] Whether or not the aliens kept this promise would prove a massive digression. The point are the parallels, time frame, and nature of contact knowing that NHI or human contactees may intentionally deceive or embellish. There remains a question of god–human copulation or an extension of Norse mythological thinking as an allegoric reprise, that the gods interacted with mortals establishing heroic or royal lineages.

Zret, who Coe initially assumed was human, had not revealed his identity when they first met, when Coe rescued Zret from rough terrain after an apparent crash landing. Because Coe helped the visitor to return to his "airplane," they entered into a friendship of great love and affection. They reconnected face to face after a period of six months initiated by a letter signed by "Xretism."[6] They met at a hotel. Thereafter, the being was known as "Zret" and it was revealed Xretism was "mister X spelled backwards."[7] Mister X was the alien's secret earth name, and he also taught Coe technological aspects of his spacecraft. Of course, this sounds ludicrous — until we consider Stevens's poem "An Exercise for Professor X" written between 1913–1915. "Dolls" precedes this poem: recall "And of Another, whom I must not name."[8] In between, "L'Essor Saccadé" (the jerky ride) presents us with a flight "over the stones of the brook, / along the stony water. / Fly over the widow's house."[9] In "Professor X," the subject matter is quite abstract. Recalling the "caliph" from

---

4 Wallace Stevens, *Collected Poetry and Prose* (The Library of America, 1997), 517.
5 Coe, *The Shocking Truth*, 89.
6 Ibid., 2.
7 Ibid., 15–16.
8 Stevens, *Collected Poetry and Prose*, 517.
9 Ibid., 219.

"Dolls," it remarks of a camel and seems to counter-instruct a "Persian":

> I see a camel in my mind.
> I do not say to myself, in English,
> "There is a camel."
> I do not talk to myself.
> On the contrary, I watch
> And a camel passes in my mind.
> This might happen to a Persian.
> My mind and a Persian's
> Are as much alike, then,
> As moonlight on the Atlantic
> Is like moonlight on the Pacific.[10]

At first, these connections feel strained. Consider however, "Headache," which is part of the series:

> I have lived so long with the rhetoricians
> That when I see a pine tree
> Broken by lightening
> Or hear a crapulous crow
> In dead boughs
> In April […]
> It is for this the rhetoricians
> Wear long black equali
> When they are abroad.[11]

Does the rhetorician reference "X"? The following stanza suggests a wanton reunion:

> It moves about, quietly
> And attentively.
> Its old hands touch me.

---

10 Ibid.
11 Ibid., 520.

Its breath touches me.
But sometimes its breath is a little cold,
Just a little,
And I know
That it is only the night wind.[12]

The role of "X" does neither end there nor is an insistence of "they." For example, in "The Creations of Sound," from *Transport to Summer* (1947):

If the poetry of X was music,
So that it came to him of its own,
Without understanding, out of the wall

Or in the ceiling, in sounds not chosen,
Or chosen quickly, in a freedom
That was their element, we should not know

That X is an obstruction, a man
Too exactly himself, and that there are words
Better without an author, without a poet,

Or having a separate author, a different poet,
An accretion from ourselves, intelligent
Beyond intelligence, an artificial man[13]

The first half of this poem concerns "their element" which permeates the room. X is not human and physical barriers won't obstruct. The element is irrational, for to convene with X requires "an accretion from ourselves," a growth. How does accretion develop? Note the tension between human and "the obstruction." Next, the apparatus of the poet which engages an irrational X: a poetic mechanism facilitates or attempts a dialogue. Was this initially a monologue of recall, as with the poems

---

12 Ibid., 521.
13 Ibid., 274–75.

of 1913–1915, such as "Dolls" and "Yellow Afternoon"? Recall that the imagination would only transform the content of missing time inadvertently triggered or recalled; that is, if it were triggered by a statue or wherever poetic energy could be found. Here a commutative capacity has increased by the technological dynamic of poetry which seeks to overcome incommensurability:

> At a distance, a secondary expositor,
> A being of sound, whom one does not approach
> Through any exaggeration. From him, we collect.
>
> Tell X that speech is not dirty silence
> Clarified. It is silence made still dirtier.
> It is more than an imitation for the ear.[14]

The secondary expositor, or one who displays music, that "being of sound" is communicating or attempting to interface speech. There is a desire to overcome incommensurability here, between X and poet:

> He lacks this venerable complication.
> His poems are not of the second part of life.
> They do not make the visible a little hard[15]

The beings do not have poetry. A "second part of life" which is the metaphysical imagination, perhaps:

> To see nor, reverberating, eke out the mind
> On peculiar horns, themselves eked out
> By the spontaneous particulars of sound.

---

14 Ibid., 275.
15 Ibid.

We do not say ourselves like that in poems.
We say ourselves in syllables that rise
From the floor, rising in speech we do not speak.[16]

The poem concludes not with a transcendental leveling; rather, an immanent experience, coasting over a real from which an exterior of language is known "from the floor," summoning a liminal barrier or membrane, an in-between the ideal of any notion of which we could speak. It is beyond the floor. The poet seems to acknowledge a possible metalanguage, the non-rendered substance of universal cosmic consciousness. A notable remark is found in *Harmonium*. "Anecdote of Canna" provides a simpler comparison:

> Huge are the canna in the dreams of
> X, the mighty thought, the mighty man.
> They fill the terrace of his capitol.
>
> His thought sleeps not. Yet thought that wakes
> In sleep may never meet another thought
> Or thing.... Now day-break comes....
>
> X promenades the dewy stones,
> Observes the canna with a clinging eye,
> Observes and then continues to observe.[17]

Coe recalls Zret describing the "City of Norma" purportedly located in Tau Ceti, the alien's home:

> The ribbon like lines that interlace the countryside are, in simple terminology, "highways" over which glide their wheelless vehicles [...] as we hover motionless, seven hundred feet above the surface [...] you can see the buildings of the city terracing down the hillsides [...] circular, with tinted

---

16 Ibid.
17 Ibid., 44.

> domed roofs and walls of pinkish white stone [...] enhanced
> with graceful curving arches and splashing fountains, amid
> a profusion of flowers, each one decorated with banners and
> colored streamers, in honor of this gala event.[18]

Poems of the 1920s which follow "Anecdote" remark of celestial beings and the perplexity of the incommensurable the poet attempts to overcome, such as "Of the Manner of Addressing Clouds": "Gloomy grammarians in golden gowns, / Meekly you keep the mortal rendezvous"; the speech of the beings "are like a music so profound"; and "exaltation without sound. / Funest philosophers and ponderers, / Their evocations are the speech of clouds. / So speech of your processional returns [...] You are to be accompanied by more / Than mute bare splendors of sun and moon."[19] This poem is followed by "Of Heaven Considered as a Tomb" which begins this way:

> What word have you, interpreters, of men
> Who in the tomb of heaven walk by night,
> The darkened ghosts of our old comedy?[20]

In *Uncollected Poems,* "Hieroglyphica" (1934) shows an italicized X returned: "*X understands Aristotle / Instinctively, not otherwise. / Hey-di-ho.*"[21] Curiously, Coe remarks on Zret's thoughts on Aristotle among other figures found in Stevens's poems such as "Vesuvius."[22] Poems of the 1940s present a non-italicized X, for example, "Someone Puts a Pineapple Together": "Himself, may be, the irreducible X / At the bottom of imagined artifice"[23];

---

18 Coe, *The Shocking Truth,* 65.
19 Stevens, *Collected Poetry and Prose,* 44–45.
20 Ibid., 45.
21 Ibid., 562. Perhaps the X of "Anecdote" was an editorial decision in the early poems? X in the later verse uses roman type, which may or may not directly mean "professor X." See also "On an Old Horn," in ibid., 211.
22 See the poem "Esthétique du Mal" for Stevens's treatment of Vesuvius. Ibid., 277.
23 Ibid., 693.

and Poem XIII of "An Ordinary Evening in New Haven": "He is neither priest nor proctor at low eve, / Under the birds, among the perilous owls, / In the big X of the returning primitive."[24] The "old comedy" and the comedian in general, are they apparitions of the past, an NHI which manifest in Coe and Stevens, unravelling in nuance through their world views?

One can only answer with speculation, that their somewhat congruent narratives and figures are a matter of communication at the level of the unbridled psyche, ungrounded as it seems beyond the technology of print. This may example degrees of deception and, in Stevens, an attempt to crack it. Here the poet deals with "Another, whom I must not name." If he was unsatisfied with the primitives, those old gods or lords of the pre-ancient world, the comedians, as it were, he probes and probes, attempting to intellectually overcome the incommensurable.

---

24 Ibid., 405.

6

The Emergence of Abstraction

> Mr. Lewis says poetry has to do with matter that is foreign
> and alien. It is never familiar to us in the way in which Plato
> wished the conquests of the mind to be familiar. On the
> contrary its function, the need which it meets and which
> has to be met in some way in every age that is not to become
> decadent or barbarous, is precisely this contact with reality as
> it impinges upon us from outside, the sense that we can touch
> and feel a solid reality which does not wholly dissolve itself
> into the conceptions of our own minds. It is the individual and
> particular that does this.
>
> — Wallace Stevens[1]

Two Intelligences

By late 1935, Wallace Stevens had reached his mid-fifties. For the next twenty years until his death, he develops a theory of poetry through studies of philosophy, art, psychology, and letters, privately at work and in his attic retreat at home.[2] The early theory

---

[1] Wallace Stevens, *Collected Poetry and Prose* (The Library of America, 1997) 701.

[2] In correspondence with William Van O'Connor, Stevens remained unsatisfied: "My prose is not what it ought to be. […] The lectures were well enough as lectures, notwithstanding all this compromise. There is

was discussed through a series of letters with then publisher Ronald Lane Latimer. When Latimer questions if art should be didactic, Stevens supplies a curious answer: "A good many people think that I am didactic. I don't want to be. My real danger is not didacticism, but abstraction, and abstraction looks very much like didacticism."[3] Abstraction was not an "aesthetic catechism" or any "initial" step to religious teaching, it concerned lived experience over a supposed ideal:

> If one could truly play the role of poet with all the books, giving one's lifetime to it, leading the special life that a poet should lead, reaching out after every possible experience, questions of this sort [intentional didacticism] would be commonplaces. They are, in fact, commonplaces now, but I am dealing with my own experience. I think that things come both from within and from without.[4]

Beyond a didactic perception why is abstraction dangerous? If not playing poet, what "experience" was he "dealing with"? To what extent was his experience understood? "I feel very much like the boy whose mother told him to stop sneezing […] 'I am not sneezing, it's sneezing me.'"[5] Conversely, Stevens is talking to a publisher and only recently has returned to verse; there may be uncertainties or ego at play. Regardless, abstraction is the original concept of a later "supreme fiction," to which he would append change, pleasure, and in a series of late letters with critic Robert Pack, whether or not *"It Must Be Human."*[6]

Stevens was uniquely unguarded with Latimer. Moreover, it's the mid-1930s and the world was changing socially and

---

nothing I desire more intensely than to make a contribution to the theory of poetry. […] If there is a great non-existent or inaccessible subject which badly needs attention, it is the theory of poetry." Holly Stevens, ed., *Letters of Wallace Stevens* (University of California Press, 1966), 585 (no. 640).

3 Ibid., 302 (no. 336).
4 Ibid.
5 Ibid.
6 Ibid., 863–64 (no. 955).

politically—to fascism, socialism, and capitalism. Unsurprisingly, Latimer queries about social order.[7] However, ideological politics seem a secondary concern. Instead, Stevens remarks on "poetic value" and the "orderly relations of society" thus rejects "one more romantic evasion in place of [...] thinking it out," which he admittedly hasn't done.[8] Such is followed by a key statement: "poetry must limit itself in respect to intelligence."[9] Moreover, "[t]here is a point at which intelligence destroys poetry."[10] Poetry, in other words, is limited not by human intelligence, but rather "the intelligence."[11] Human intelligence and prescribed social order seem to obfuscate progress. It's a rather strong statement and perhaps why Stevens reverts to speculation:

> Possibly the point at which intelligence is inimical is a movable point. Everyone realizes that now-a-days we are a good deal more exacting about the meaning of poetry than we used to be.
>
> Whether internal order proceeds from external order, or the other way round, is something that I think I must have spoken of in an earlier letter. For my own part, I think that everything has its origin in externals.[12]

---

7 In the Alfred Knopf edition of *Ideas of Order* (1936), Stevens's statement on the dust jacket concerns ideas of a "different nature" than those of political and social order. Namely "the dependence of the individual, confronting the elimination of established ideas." Stevens, *Collected Poetry and Prose*, 997.

8 Stevens, *Letters of Wallace Stevens*, 305 (no. 339).

9 Ibid.

10 Ibid.

11 Stevens's use of "the intelligence" can be found in "Man Carrying Thing," which in my view clarifies prior exchanges with Latimer about inimicality (Stevens, *Collected Poetry and Prose*, 306). In other words, that intelligence is inimical leads to distinction by way of "the," which is further substantiated in the prose "The Figure of the Youth as Virile Poet": "the incandescence of the intelligence" (ibid., 680). See also the final stanza of "The Man on the Dump" (ibid., 185).

12 Stevens, *Letters of Wallace Stevens*, 305 (no. 339).

Order is originally of an external concerning *the intelligence* as such — everything. How else to interpret this? For the individual, something happens from without and something responds from within; this drives Stevens's concept of abstraction. The poet invents a way to order individual experience of reality upon the realization human intelligence is limited by an external force. In other words, the intelligence renders human probing inimical; it cannot contravene and is perpetually deceived.

The without and within form a contradiction — if not a chiastic X — between *human* intelligence and the intelligence, or "the loss of language creates confusion or dumbness"[13]; and, even more so, "poetry must resist the intelligence almost successfully."[14] These are contradictions we all can relate to, as those in power tend to wield them. A politician lies but may pass worthy legislation. A clergyman will sin but equally give comfort. The scientist haunted by natural mystery seeks to convert phenomena into factual truths, doing so by subjective means for objective ends. What's different for the poet is a compulsion to express as if there are no other options. One might be tempted to claim they know why they were sneezing. Yet even if defining a place in the literary market to Latimer, I find deeper trepidation more than posturing. For example:

> If poetry introduces order, and every competent poem introduces order, and if order means peace, even though that particular peace is an illusion, is it any less an illusion than a good many other things that everyone high and low now-a-days concedes to be no longer of any account? Isn't a freshening of life a thing of consequence? It would be a great thing to change the status of the poet.[15]

It seems the intelligence as poetry leads him to an apolitical yet heroic purpose stopping short of his own chiastic crucifixion:

---

13 Stevens, *Collected Poetry and Prose*, 901.
14 Ibid., 910.
15 Stevens, *Letters of Wallace Stevens*, 293 (no. 329).

> There is no reason why any poet should not have the status of the philosopher, nor why his poetry should not give up to the keenest minds and the most searching spirits something of what philosophy gives up and, in addition, the peculiar things that only poetry can give.[16]

The poet must stand equal then, be recognized as more, but why? This seems to contradict the didactic posture he wanted to avoid.[17] Thus "poetry itself," if accepted as the intelligence, elects one to overcome impasses with an exclusive peculiarity.[18] If our intelligence is inimical, he has the answer — paradox solved and power as a poet established. Yet would this not be an illusion of peace? If wanted from Latimer was a reconsideration of poetry's public or political value, it's difficult to parse from egoism. Nonetheless, Stevens was ensconced by a unique "danger," an original experience "from without" carried within. Thus, one way to overcome this would be through a "competent poem"[19] — originally driven by an intelligence which is not local. If the within is a growing awareness of missing time, abstraction is essential to overcoming an individual's inimical limit regarding the without.

Abstraction and Method

Through abstraction the irrational element — unthought order from without — is rendered by the reason. Such is later characterized as the "methodizer" of the imagination.[20] An early example comes when reviewing "Owl's Clover": "It is difficult for me to think and not to think abstractly. Consequently; in

---

16 Ibid., 292 (no. 329).
17 Stevens, *Collected Poetry and Prose*, 864.
18 "Poetry itself" first appears in the mid-1930s in Stevens, "Sur Plusieurs Beaux Sujects," in *Collected Poetry and Prose*, 916. He mentions it as early as 1899 but offers no definition. Stevens, *Letters of Wallace Stevens*, 26 (no. 26).
19 Stevens, *Letters of Wallace Stevens*, 293 (no. 328).
20 Stevens, *Collected Poetry and Prose*, 738.

order to avoid abstractness, in writing, I search out instinctively things that express the abstract and yet are not in themselves abstractions."[21] The statue central to "Owl's Clover" he termed a "variable symbol." This symbol, the statue, is a triggering object found instinctively—not intentionally. Stevens complains to Latimer this was misunderstood in a recent review. There the statue "is also a symbol, but not specifically a symbol for art; its use has been somewhat broadened and, so far as I have defined it at all, it is a symbol for things as they are. [... M]y object in all this is simply to write poetry, keeping it as true as possible to myself and as near as possible to the idea that I have in mind."[22] Variable symbol "as far as I have defined it" suggests uncertainty regarding what was encountered. At base, the statue enables abstraction to unfold whatever is retained within. The poem captures variations of the seed memory, originally a matter of without as discussed in Chapters Three and Four.

By late 1935, Stevens's poetic method involves free association and instinct, which I associate with abstraction, that is, how one's inimical limit might be overcome following notions of intelligence:

> [T]he explanation for the bursts of freedom is nothing more than this: that when one is thinking one's way the pattern becomes small and complex, but when one has reached a point and finds it possible to move emotionally one goes ahead rapidly. One of the most difficult things in writing poetry is to know what one's subject is. Most people know what it is and do not write poetry, because they are so conscious of that one thing. One's subject is always poetry, or should be. But sometimes it becomes a little more definite and fluid, and then the thing goes ahead rapidly.[23]

---

21 Stevens, *Letters of Wallace Stevens*, 290 (no. 328).
22 Ibid., 290–91 (no. 328).
23 Stevens, *Letters of Wallace Stevens*, 297 (no. 331).

THE EMERGENCE OF ABSTRACTION

By early 1936, motive is refined by a distinction between "poetry of the subject" and the "true subject" as iterated months before in "The Irrational Element in Poetry."[24] Writes Stevens to Latimer:

> The truth is that egotism is at the bottom of everything everybody does, and that, if some really acute observer made as much of egotism as Freud has made of sex, people would forget a good deal about sex and find the explanation for everything in egotism. I write poetry because I want to write it. We are likely to give many incorrect explanations for what we do instinctively. It is very easy for me to say that I write poetry in order to formulate my ideas and to relate myself to the world. That is why I think I write it, though it may not be the right reason. That being so, I think that I should continue to write poetry whether or not anybody ever saw it, and certainly I write lots of it that nobody ever sees. We are all busy thinking things that nobody ever knows about.[25]

As noted at the end of Chapter One, Stevens's "poetic order" means the "coordination of the poetic aspects of the world." Such aspects are linked through poetic function; a within which drives the poet to coordinate its dispersion without. (This dovetails Dante's want of Beatrice which triggers a Jungian apotropaic circle, as noted in Chapter Two.) Abstraction therefore involves an initial instinctive which eventually informs a willful if not desirous action. Thus, if human intelligence is inimical when attempting to contravene the intelligence, a poet's task is to move toward commensurability with the praeternatural — to render, not suppress, variable symbols or notions of the absolute object. For there are superior laws, logics, and language we insist are irrational — which is tantamount to our own repression.[26]

The abstraction of missing time was clearly underway by the 1930s, over time it moves from an *instinctive sneezing* into desire

---

24 Stevens, *Collected Poetry and Prose*, 785–87.

25 "Egoism." Stevens, *Letters of Wallace Stevens*, 306 (no. 340).

26 Stevens, *Collected Poetry and Prose*, 738.

for a theoretic. Abstraction had no such quality at the end of the first awakening. For example, on March 27, 1922, Stevens writes a letter to Alice Corbin Henderson:

> My poems seem so simple and natural to me that I am never able to understand how they may seem otherwise to anyone else. They are not intended to be either deep, dark or mysterious. Whatever can be expressed can be expressed clearly. Epater les savants is as trifling as épater les bourgeois. But one cannot always say a thing clearly and retain the poetry of what one is saying. For instance, at the moment I am writing a thing called Palace of the Blondes Who Read Books of Moonlight. Now that means precisely what it says. If I said: this poem is a momentary cure for poverty; it raises a class to its highest exponent, to the satisfaction of its imagination of what it would like to be; it inflames and placates desire—and so on, I should convey the same idea but I should not write a poem. Now, the disbeliever in the Palace of the Babies is the mood of the disenchanted in the presence of the enchanted (I hate like the devil to write like this).[27]

This explanation appears before *Harmonium*. As to the poem "Palace of the Babies," specifically in regard to the believer/disbeliever, what's implied by "I hate like the devil to write like this?" If he dislikes "enchanted," why permit the 1921 publication in *Poetry Magazine* and once again in *Harmonium*? Perhaps he does not like explaining his poetry, hence his stance against didacticism. Yet the declaration "whatever can be expressed" is consistent with later remarks in 1935; that if the only emphasis is a specific subject, say poverty, then what one does is not poetry—it's too small and complex. A predecessor to the true subject is also apparent, namely "what seems natural to me," which arrives from free association—free-moving and emotional. Therefore, by the 1920s, why one writes poetry is a natu-

---

27 Stevens, *Collected Poetry and Prose*, 937–38. This letter does not appear in *The Letters of Wallace Stevens*.

ral mystery. A decade later, abstraction matures along with his idea of "poetic order." It comes to this: if whatever one writes follows the true subject, the poetry of the subject is permissible if merely accidental. The true subject, which the poetry of the subject retains retrospectively, discloses hence reorders what's missing back into conscious awareness. Recall from "Man with The Blue Guitar: "An absence in reality, / Things as they are. Or so we say."[28] The next stanza in poem XXII reveals a culmination, a questioning of naivety: "But are these separate?" and that "absence for the poem [...] acquires [...] true appearances" through a circuitry or "universal intercourse."[29] Therefore, the truth of poetic "fact" unifies a disjunction of experience (the ordering of absences, else missing time) as self-disclosure.[30] The poem discloses what *the intelligence* did not originally permit through inimical probing. This leads to the first tenant of supreme fiction: *It Must Be Abstract*.

Does the Henderson letter reveal any political or moral ideation? The *scholar* and the *bourgeois* are equivocated and he need not impress. Recall that if "most people know what it is," it means "they do not write poetry." Stevens's potential insincerity concerns his publicly stated intent of "Owl's Clover": It may be cross-referenced with not being "a cure for poverty" regarding "Palace of the Blondes Who Read Books of Moonlight" (a curiously named poem which does not exist beyond the title). Insincerity, in other words, concerning "Owl's Clover," is particular to the subsection "The Old Woman and the Statue" or what he reads and remarks upon in "The Irrational Element in Poetry":

> To be specific, I wanted to apply my own sensibility to something perfectly matter-of-fact. The result would be a disclosure of my own sensibility or individuality, as I called it a moment ago, certainly to myself. The poem is called "The Old Woman and the Statue." The old woman is a symbol of

---

28 Stevens, *Collected Poetry and Prose*, 145.
29 Ibid.
30 On "(absolute) fact," see ibid., 679–81.

> those who suffered during the depression and the statue is a symbol of art, although in several poems of which *Owl's Clover,* the book from which I shall read, consists, the statue is a variable symbol.[31]

Here one detects more didactic danger when explaining abstraction. Curious, for what follows is a strange comment on how the content of verse is distributed through a "poetic mechanism":

> While there is nothing automatic about the poem, nevertheless it has an automatic aspect in the sense that it is what I wanted it to be without knowing before it was written what I wanted it to be, even though I knew before it was written what I wanted to do. If each of us is a biological mechanism, each poet is a poetic mechanism. To the extent that what he produces is mechanical: that is to say, beyond his power to change, it is irrational. Perhaps I do not mean wholly beyond his power to change, for he might, by an effort of the will, change it.[32]

Thus, poetic energy or potency "wherever [...] it is to be found"[33] denotes the predominance of conscious energy over materialistic ideation. Utilizing this element, the recovery of missing time is attained from free association, a type of self-hypnosis or meditation. Whether or not it can change what comes about depends upon the will to follow the ordering of what is disclosed. However, missing time is originally irrational and must be accepted if what is produced is mechanical and beyond our ability to *change* it (sneezing, or the apprehending of apperceptions).

Broadly considered, abstraction accesses not only the triggering statue or object, it sources an outside ledger of consciousness, a negative in terms of materialist or naturalist dogma; the nether of consciousness or psychic substance. What abstraction

---

31 Ibid., 783–84.
32 Ibid., 784.
33 Ibid., 783.

permits is the growth of individual intelligence surpassing a naïve or inimical posture. This I believe is central to Stevens's consternation with the official view of being. The irrational is thus a responsibility which informs the poet's commitments for psychical progress. Yet when facing it, one may not have a word for it. In other words, the irrational defines Stevens's ground or what's usually construed as political insensitivity, aloofness, or indifference. For one, the irrational concerns absences in our conscious reality. Because it is an element, the irrational retains a potential of intellectual expansion. (A term used for this is "region" as discussed in Chapter Two.) If we do not accede, we simply argue about lesser degrees of a general illusion. Therefore, ideological views are necessarily myopic, small, and complex; if lacking a better account of a sufficient cause. Second, our eventual knowledge of the irrational is otherwise invested in the poem and distributed globally. Following the irrational intends for the true subject's incipience, once a natural mystery cyphered in verse. Third, such is disclosed through retrospection of poetry which, by the irrational element, fuels a world change-dynamic—the point is to take pleasure. Such engenders more poetry and is part of the poet's desire. This incessant production is ontologically transmogrifying. Radical individuality is the inevitable outcome. After all, answers often arrive before questions, titles before books. If not alien politics, it is certainly alienation from the illusions that most stubbornly embrace. The moment one realizes they are weirder than most is an alien feeling. That is all one needs to know about politics.

Transmogrification

The poet's subjectification is not an imposed or repressive change from above any more than from below. It is simply a dynamic between the without and within. The intelligence permeates the body and transforms their psychical range. The body is an antenna of mind, a dimensionless surface, a membrane of distributed carbonic energy. An image of transmogrification is present in "Owl's Clover." Stevens's abstractions of the statue demonstrate the variable symbol which disclose sensibility and individuality:

> The statue is the sculptor not the stone.
> In this he carved himself, he carved his age,
> He carved the feathery walkers standing by,
> Twitching a little with crude souvenirs
> Of young identities, Aprilian stubs.
> Exceeding sex, he touched another race,
> Above our race, yet of ourselves transformed,[34]

Here the poet inscribes himself in things or, once more, is facing the absolute object. Is this statue alive? Clearly the material is not the maker yet he carved himself. Additionally, consider "another race, / Above our race, yet of ourselves transformed," one that "he touched," which exceeds sex. Does this recount the high strangeness of the Angel of the Waters statue in Central Park from February 1901? Was it reconceived as "the necessary angel," as found in "Angel Surrounded by Paisans," a late poem which depicts a fleeting experience with a non-human entity?[35] What about the shift from disbeliever to believer in "Palace of the Babies"?[36] In the Henderson letter, he links "Palace of the Blondes Who Read Books of Moonlight" to this poem. It is likely "The Ordinary Women" is what becomes of "Palace of the Blondes Who Read Books of Moonlight," which begins this way: "Then from their poverty they rose, / From dry catarrhs, and to guitars / They flitted / Through the palace walls."[37] Reading the entire poem, it implies working women and his reconsideration suggests intelligent deception. It carries hallmarks of a recollected dream and seems to present the scenery of a brothel. This would be the poetry of the subject: *women of poverty selling their bodies,* but we now know the true subject concerns *the intel-*

---

34 Ibid., 165.
35 Ibid., 423.
36 Ibid., 61.
37 Ibid., 8.

THE EMERGENCE OF ABSTRACTION

ligence which defers inimical probing. "Blondes" means not to uplift anyone impoverished who may read it — he writes poetry for himself. Thus, an orderly distribution regards the beginning stanza which ends nearly the same — a poem which resolves tension between a man and intelligent deception. Nonetheless, it must be abstracted.[38]

Yet there is a connection between "Palace of the Babies" whose "disbeliever walked the moonlit place"[39] with the "Palace of the Blondes Who Read Books of Moonlight" ironically retitled "The Ordinary Women" — and this fact, should it be true, means to return the poem back to the true subject. For such women flit through walls, in other words, walk through solid material presumedly in whatever a "palace" could be. In abduction scholarship, beings who pass through walls are reported by experiencers who themselves do so either willfully or in a captive, trance state. Moreover, "Blondes" concerns an inflaming and placating of desire. Such invites a suspicion of NHI copulation and psychical transformation. There are other suggestions of visiting beings in a similar way such as "The Silver Plough-Boy,"[40] "The Apostrophe to Vincintine,"[41] and "Disillusionment of Ten O'Clock."[42] Note here that the disquiet in these instances concerns separation. In abduction scholarship, babies are often incubated in glass-like containers. Such a scene is described by John Mack in "Peter's Story" which is astoundingly similar to parts of Stevens's poems:

> Outside now Peter looked down. "I realize that I'm floating, and I see the ground. I see the side of the house... I see the ship above us," he said, "and I make my way towards it," and "next I'm in the ship." Inside "all the babies are there, all the

---

[38] To note, the poem "The Ordinary Women" ends with a homophonic shift between "guitar" and "catarrhs." That is the only difference between opening and closing stanzas. Ibid., 8.

[39] Ibid., 61.

[40] Ibid., 42.

[41] Ibid.

[42] Ibid., 52.

children are there." He was standing in a room that was black, "like black marble or something." Along a curving wall of a corridor that seemed like the outer perimeter of the ship, there were little lights at about hip level.[43]

Recall that in "Palace of the Babies" our poet walks a moonlit place where "hammered serafin" mark a gate's entrance thus "Observing moon-blotches on the walls." There's a yellow light "rocked across the still façades, / Or else say spinning on the pinnacles, / While he imagined humming sounds and sleep." The blank windows of this building suggest a structure or craft. Thus a shimmering room speculating "If in" where the "babies came, / Drawn close by dreams of fledgling wing, / It was because night nursed them in its fold."[44] The doubled serafin occurs in the night, or withdraws and brings a type of night. Night personification means he's "drawn close" by another being. Solitude remarks of an intimate connection lost, the poet sinks into the mystery within, but retains the notion of an extraordinary without — a transformation carried by the poems. For example, in "The Ordinary Women" beings "crowded / The nocturnal halls," and moonlight "fubbed the girandoles" or wall mounted candle fixtures with mirrors similar to hall lights in Peter's story. The women "read right long" and "The moonlight / Rose on the beachy floors", thus

> Insinuations of desire,
> Puissant speech, alike in each,
> Cried quittance
> To the wickless halls.[45]

---

[43] For comparison see "Peter's story" in John E. Mack, *Abduction: Human Encounters with Aliens* (Scribner, 1994) 320–23. Also "Peter Khoury" in Richard M. Dolan, *UFOs for the 21st Century Mind: The Definitive Guide to the UFO Mystery: New and Expanded Edition* (Richard Dolan Press, 2023), 311.

[44] Stevens, *Collected Poetry and Prose*, 61.

[45] Ibid., 8–9.

Abstraction pulls from the subconscious and is reconfigured within the poet's milieux, whatever that happens to be by way of free association and peripheral refractions. Whatever it happens to be was not entirely obvious to Stevens by the early 1920s. This suggests NHI cognizance is embedded within the poem, which protects if not shields the human from "the shocking truth," as Coe put it, or rather ontological shock, as we know it today. Concerning transmogrification, whatever Stevens encounters in the early years clearly changed him. If he didn't know why he wrote poetry, he would remain unsatisfied with conventional explananda. A poem, it seems, withholds or attains consciousness once spirited away only to disclose reality in mortal time. Theory, in other words, names this "abstraction" insofar as it returns something lost from conscious experience. Disclosure provides what was retained in content form as absence. The poem is therefore a divine apparatus interwoven with an "incandescence of the intelligence" which it brings transmogrifying the body further into mind.[46]

A Note on Involuntary Memory

When the poet follows the orb in "Owl's Clover," it leads him to a stunning scene. He finds dwarves but also levitates above them:

> The portent would become man-haggard to
> A race of dwarfs, the meditative arms
> And head a shadow trampled under hoofs,
> Man-misty to a race star-humped, astride
> In a clamor thudding up from central earth.
> Not the space in camera of the man below,
> Immeasurable, the space in which he knows
> The locust's titter and the turtle's sob.
> The statue stands in true perspective. Crows
> Give only their color to the leaves. The trees

---

[46] Ibid., 680.

> Are full of fanfares of farewell, as night
> And the portent end in night, composed, before
> Its wheel begins to turn.[47]

I surmised that the merger of Stevens's milieux with the statue occurs at the level of involuntary memory. A plausible theorization of abstraction and recall can be drawn from Walter Benjamin, who applied such to Charles Baudelaire's lyric poetry. This he defined "in Proustian terms [...] that only what has not been experienced explicitly and consciously, what has not happened to the subject as an isolated experience [*Erlebnis*], can become a component of *mémoire involontaire*."[48] How might the Angels of the Waters figure have entered into the element of the involuntary only to be triggered by the variable symbol of "Owl's Clover"?[49] Writes Benjamin:

> If we think of the associations which, at home in the *mémoire involontaire,* seek to cluster around an object of perception, and if we call those associations the aura of that object, then the aura attaching to the object of a perception corresponds precisely to the experience [*Erfahrung*] which, in the case of an object of use, inscribes itself as long practice. The techniques inspired by the camera and subsequent analogous types of apparatus extend the range of the *mémoire involontaire;* these techniques make it possible at any time to retain an event — as image and sound — through the apparatus.[50]

---

47 Ibid., 170.
48 Walter Benjamin, "On Some Motifs in Baudelaire," in *Walter Benjmain Selected Writings,* vol. 4, 1938–1940: *Fruits of Exile,* eds. Howard Eiland, Michael W. Jennings, trans. Edmund Jepchott (Belknap Press of Harvard University Press, 2003), 317.
49 I refer here to Stevens's adventure in Central Park as documented in his journals. See Chapter Three of this book.
50 Benjamin, "On Some Motifs in Baudelaire," 337.

If the poem is a subjectification technology, "long practice" facilitates a recall: "In this he carved himself."[51] Accordingly, Freud's *Pleasure Principle* equivocates the protection and reception of stimuli. The parity of a "protective shield" is consequential of "shock" or a rupture that initially neutralizes stimuli from recognition. Continues Benjamin:

> "The impressions and sense perceptions of humans," [Paul] Valery writes, "actually belong in the category of surprises; they are evidence of an insufficiency in humans ... Recollection is ... an elemental phenomenon which aims at giving us the time for organizing 'the reception of stimuli' which we initially lacked." The reception of shocks is facilitated by training in coping with stimuli; if need be, dreams as well as recollection may be enlisted. As a rule, however — so Freud assumes — this training devolves upon the wakeful consciousness, located in a part of the cortex which is "so frayed by the effect of the stimulus" that it offers the most favorable situation for the reception of stimuli. That the shock is thus cushioned, parried by consciousness, would lend the incident that occasions it the character of an isolated experience [*Erlebnis*], in the strict sense. If it were incorporated directly in the register of conscious memory, it would sterilize this incident for poetic experience [*Erfahrung*].[52]

Order and poetry are afoot here — precisely poetic function derived from an "elemental phenomenon" wherefrom poetic experience abstracts what was intially sterilized. Moreover, the surprise can be compared to Stevens's free association, which allows for an orderly distribution when aligned with the true subject of the poem; a truth of the intelligence which otherwise occults conscious experience of a contactee. Poetic experience is thus a disclosing of the real as an unreal which takes flight in the idealism of metaphysical thought. Of a real, its capacity sits

---

51 Stevens, *Collected Poetry and Prose*, 165.
52 Benjamin, "On Some Motifs in Baudelaire," 317–19.

behind the metaphysical imagination, in wait for recall; willfully as retrospective self-disclosure. The poem links the arcane to human spacetime. The irrational element provides this capacity as a reality secondarily found as unreality when disclosed in whatever way it may be. We miss reality, in other words, if dismissing it as the unreal. Thus, there may be a counter-sterilization by the imagination (if not sterilized then coopted by "the intelligence") which has the capacity to critique the suppression of conscious experience through a terrestrial or human world intelligence. This concerns what Stevens calls "the imagination as metaphysics."[53] And here recall that "potent subject" which "critiques the irrational" when it "comes to be written" by "whomever it may be that this potent subject ultimately engages."[54]

The poem is an abstractor and protector of unofficial reality, softening the blow of an ontological shock which emerges as a naïve metaphysical posture. In this way, the statue takes the status of "an absolute object" as it orders the content of a poem for a later disclosure of its global distribution. The reports of its aura, in other words, are wake waves of a supreme dialogue, of *psyche materialis* disclosing to the self. Thus order, poetry's task to establish peace, makes manifest the ordering sacrality of the statue. After all, there is a desire ignited in the encounter of the statue, which pulls upon involuntary memory originally shocked from view.[55] The apparatuses of capture inform long experience; they are mechanisms which critique an otherwise unadulterated, irrational element. Poetry informs the basis of technological capture and teaches us disclosure through the existent self.

---

53 Stevens, *Collected Poetry and Prose*, 726.
54 Ibid., 792.
55 Benjamin, "On Some Motifs in Baudelaire," 337–38.

7

The Affirmation of John Mack

It is the human that is the alien,
The human that has no cousin in the moon.

— Wallace Stevens[1]

Psychological Poetics

At the end of Wallace Stevens's "The Irrational Element in Poetry," we are presented with the following prognostication: "It will be time enough to adopt a more systematic usage, when the critique of the irrational comes to be written, by whomever it may be that this potent subject ultimately engages."[2] From this an ethics of the imagination emerges. There are two practical modes he delineates. The first is prone to extinction, the other fulfillment. Stevens challenged us to consider the imagination as primary, a passage one takes with regard to reality which informs subjective modes wherefrom a *poet of extinction* or *a poet of fulfillment* are operative; a despair poet who chooses illusion or a poet of fulfillment who accepts *reality and*

---

1 Wallace Stevens, *Collected Poetry and Prose* (The Library of America, 1997), 288.
2 Ibid., 792.

*the imagination are one.*³ If not always intentional, the poet of extinction enables destructive or repressive outcomes by applying the imagination as deception of the self or others. They insist on unreality as reality, as a final fact or total definition. Fatally, the destructive poet risks severing an awareness to what is vital or noetic in trade for fanciful artificiality. Conversely, and not always intentionally, the poet of fulfillment multiplies beauty and joy throughout unreality by an ethical, creative practice. Countercritically, the poet of fulfillment confronts an imposed artificial existence.

Throughout this book I have made reference to John E. Mack (1929–2004), an American psychiatrist, author, and professor best known for his contribution to our understanding of alien abduction. Mack rode with the poet of fulfillment. In the early 1990s he began interviewing abductees, later termed "experiencers" of the phenomenon. The result was his landmark study *Abduction: Human Encounters with Aliens* (1994), which consolidates numerous hypnotic regressions and features thirteen detailed case files. From these sessions Mack noticed consistencies which defied psychiatric norms and scientific understanding.⁴ The psychiatrist began to reconsider the dualism of "objec-

---

3   Ibid., 738.
4   From a clinical perspective, he became convinced "something that had really taken place […] what they were telling me about was not, from the standpoint of my view of reality, possible." This led to questioning his own concept of reality forged through decades of academic study and clinical practice: "Faced with a phenomenon that does not fit one's ontological perspective, the choices are to ignore it, to force it into the old mold […] or to modify or expand the worldview itself." Mack chose the latter: "Compelled by the power of the clinical evidence, I have felt that I must […] believe that the experiences are in some way real, even though they challenge my notions of reality." At the time of *Abduction,* Mack headed the department of psychiatry at Harvard Medical School since 1977, a position retained until death. The Pulitzer Prize recipient had a lot to lose and nearly did. Regardless, Mack's reception of abductees drove more questions forth: "[H]ow do we decide what is real, and, if domains of the real can be distinguished, what are the methodologies or ways of knowing appropriate to each domain?" John E. Mack, *Abduction: Human Encounters with Aliens* (Scribner, 1994), 11.

tive and subjective domains, outer and inner, which tend to be held as distinct and separate." The objective domain concerns methods of natural sciences apropos to materialism, whereas the subjective domain concerns what is otherwise anomalous "psyche or spirit" or what "we learn about [...] through consciousness itself [...] through language and art."[5] Searching for answers, Mack consulted his childhood friend, philosopher and famed author of *The Structure of Scientific Revolutions* (1962), Thomas Kuhn. Kuhn's advice was tantamount to phenomenological reduction; a methodological suspension of judgment for the necessity of rigor:

> Kuhn's observation that the Western scientific paradigm had come to assume the rigidity of a theology, and that this belief system was held in place by the structures, categories, and polarities of language, such as real/unreal, exists/does not exist, objective/subjective, intrapsychic/external world, and happened/did not happen. He suggested [...] I suspend to the degree that I was able all of these language forms and simply collect raw information, putting aside whether or not what I was learning fit any particular worldview. Later I would see what I had found and whether any coherent theoretical formulation would be possible. This, by and large, has been the approach that I have tried to follow.[6]

---

5   Ibid., 10.
6   Ibid., 23. Mack's checking of scientific dogma is wholly similar to the positions taken by famed UFO researcher Jacques Vallee, who sought for decades to understand incommensurability between nonhuman intelligences and our own. Having recognized naturalist materialism will not suffice, Vallee incorporates intelligence into his theoretical approach in want of an "existence theorem." Vallee situates metalogic as a theoretical basis for understanding UFO phenomena. His supposition that consciousness transcends "time itself" is admittedly called "absurd," yet he notes, if not insists, upon a "deeply poetic and paradoxical quality." His cursory example was unicorns. "Does a unicorn have a horn in the middle of its head — yes." "Do unicorns exists — no." Jacques Vallee, *Alien Contact Trilogy*, vol. 1: *Dimensions: A Casebook of Alien Contact* (Anomalist Books, 2003), 209.

Mack's work with experiencers mirrors the poetic function of self-disclosure. From the perspective of the ethics of the imagination, Mack takes the role of the critic who originally operates by the official view. The experiencer, through hypnosis, takes the position of poet whose testimonies are poetical, thus an unofficial view of the irrational. Experiencers provide data from which Mack determines norms and insights. The experiencer is aware of something unreal yet needs to get to a place which unlocks more of the true subject subconsciously. Mack on the other hand observes a consistent narrative. Disclosed is an abductee's affect, despair, isolation, or beguilement through regression. Thus Mack's reasoning of irrational perturbances leads to acceptance, hence fulfilment.[7] Likewise, Mack is able to redress assumptions of scientific materialism and the nature of reality. The change in subjective reality of experiencers (which undoubtedly affected him as well) Mack termed "ontological shock":

> [P]owerful feelings that came up during the session, additional memories that surfaced, and how they are managing what I call the "ontological shock" [.... A]bductees may have still clung to the possibility that these experiences are dreams or [...] mental disorder. The denial never disappears altogether, and a shock may recur, even after several hypnosis sessions.[8]

With Stevens, a thwarting of denial emerges as early as 1921, when "Palace of the Babies" was originally published. His reaction to this poem, as revealed in the Henderson letter of 1922, intimates that his shift to a believer was difficult yet inevitable. If one accepts his approach to poetry is analogous to hypnosis sessions (not the same methodologically but accessing features of the subconscious mind), the awakenings of 1910s and 1930s show a coming to terms with the reality of his unreal particular

---

7   Mack, *Abduction*, 155.
8   Ibid., 27.

but not exclusive to "The Man with the Blue Guitar" (1935) and the emergence of abstraction. The trajectory of Stevens's oeuvre follows Mack's overall assessment of an experiencer's journey. This may have developed through contact with nonhuman intelligences over several decades. To this, writes Mack:

> The alien beings that abductees speak about seem to many of them to come from another domain [...] closer to the source of being or primary creation. They have been described, however homely their appearance, as intermediaries or emissaries from God, even as angels [...]. The acknowledgment of their existence, after the initial ontological shock, is sometimes [...] the first step in the opening of consciousness to a universe that is no longer simply material. Abductees come to appreciate that the universe is filled with intelligences and is itself intelligent. They develop a sense of awe before a mysterious cosmos that becomes sacred and ensouled. The sense of separation from all the rest of creation breaks down and the experience of oneness becomes an essential aspect of the evolution of the abductee's consciousness.[9]

Angels are a feature of many of Stevens's poems as well as divinities. By point of fact, he titled his prose collection *The Necessary Angel: Essays on Reality and the Imagination* (1951). Experiencers may not be considered poets. However, they are engaged with nonhuman intelligences mentally and physically. Who is to say they would not attain or surpass the poet in the range of sensitivity or sensibility? For experiencers are compelled to move beyond the standards of materialism and naturalism. For Mack, what becomes fact are abductee experiences, leading to ontological shock if not an enlargement of his own scientific realism.

Encountering nonhuman intelligence has caused some to extend ordinary sensibility. In that way experiencers become poets, for they have *seen*. Yet prior to regression what they have seen was a pejorative unreal. Thus, when Mack receives testi-

---

9   Ibid., 410–11.

monial evidences what is beyond sensibility is also *seen*, rather, *seen* through his official status as a medical professional. If Mack encounters what Stevens terms "an incandescence of the intelligence"[10] via experiencers, he does so as the figure of the critic. Thus by *seen* we are not focusing on nuts-and-bolts proof. We are dealing with what I term primary and secondary *theōria*, a mental contemplation at the level of the imagination which is applied by Mack in his regression sessions.

Determining what is permissible as "poetic truth" was equally rigorous for Stevens. After all,

> [T]he poet must get rid of the hieratic in everything that concerns him and must move constantly in the direction of the credible. He must create his unreal out of what is real.
>
> If we consider the nature of our experience when we are in agreement with reality, we find, for one thing, we cease to be metaphysicians.[11]

Within himself Mack debased the hieratic figure of scientific dogma. Did he avoid metaphysical entrapments or simply pass through them? Perhaps. Yet he was creating an unreal out of regressions, rather, what was real to him in terms of understanding the nature of reality. Notwithstanding, his ethical concern meant to check embellishment of the incredible that needs to transition into the credible. I surmise that Mack finds what Stevens propounds that "poetic truth is factual truth"[12]; thus "only reality […] seen […] by those whose range in the perception of fact — that is, whose sensibility — is greater than our own."[13]

---

10 Stevens, *Collected Poetry and Prose*, 680.
11 Ibid., 679.
12 Ibid., 680.
13 Ibid.

From Belief to Belief: Simulation and Supreme Fiction

Stevens's journey as an experiencer may open us to reconsider Mack's conclusions about the nature of reality. Parallels to the problematic of belief and reality are found in a letter Wallace Stevens pens to a close friend in the 1940s:

> One evening, a week or so ago, a student at Trinity College came to the office and walked home with me. We talked about this book [*Notes Toward a Supreme Fiction*]. I said that I thought that we had reached a point at which we could no longer really believe in anything unless we recognized that it was a fiction. The student said that that was an impossibility, that there was no such thing as believing in something that one knew was not true. It is obvious, however, that we are doing that all the time. There are things with respect to which we willingly suspend disbelief; if there is instinctive in us a will to believe, or if there is a will to believe, whether or not it is instinctive, it seems to me that we can suspend disbelief with reference to a fiction as easily as we can suspend it with reference to anything else. There are fictions that are extensions of reality. [...] Heaven is an extension of reality.[14]

Stevens's first of four points is that *everything is fiction*. The second, there is an automatic and unquestioned belief *in this fiction* wherefrom we deem it reality. This is initially a subjective mode of an unreal, artificial world. Paradoxically, it is a world that cannot account for anything more than itself (hence the absence that poetry contrarily reveals to him). The third point is that *we believe in things* which are *not true* "all the time." This concerns a deeper awareness of artifice or fiction which imposes unwitting beliefs. It remarks of a deeper relation to the subconscious; not mere Coleridgean fancy or a closed-off, self-devouring pathology of despair. Thus the fourth point, "there are fictions that

---

14 Holly Stevens, ed., *Letters of Wallace Stevens* (University of California Press, 1966), 430 (no. 467).

are extensions of reality," declares that reality provides fictions in which we believe *willingly;* that is, accepting an original will of an otherwise quotidian, fictitious force. That one opts to use this will is a matter of spiritual advance and an ethical choice. One does so by suspending belief in unreality, which opens up to a belief apropos to reality itself (perhaps another iteration of unreality). Our access to reality is therefore an affair of confronting the simulation of belief within the unreality in which we are steeped. When we confront the authoritarian fiction of the unreal world, that mode of belief is no longer sufficient; rather, it is necessarily there. Reality is what we suspend disbelief for, thus the human world is simply one form of fiction toward supreme fiction.

Stevens's "supreme fiction" offers a theoretical development of ontological shock. Supreme fiction concerns three primary functions: It Must Be Abstract; It Must Change; It Must Give Pleasure.[15] These functions give rise to a fourth: It Must Be Human? I add a question mark for good reason. Stevens did not officially incorporate the human question into *Notes Toward a Supreme Fiction,* however, he had considered it.

It must be abstract:

> He must be able to abstract himself and also to abstract reality, which he does by placing it in his imagination.[16]

It must change:

> If it is defined, it will be fixed and it must not be fixed. As in the case of an external thing, nobility resolves itself into an enormous number of vibrations, movements, changes. To fix it is to put an end to it. Let me show it to you unfixed.[17]

---

15 Stevens, *Collected Poetry and Prose,* 329–52.
16 Ibid., 657.
17 Ibid., 664.

It must give pleasure:

> The pleasure is the pleasure of powers that create a truth that cannot be arrived at by the reason alone, a truth that the poet recognizes by sensation. The morality of the poet's radiant and productive atmosphere is the morality of the right sensation.[18]

It must be human?:

> For a long time, I have thought of adding other sections to the NOTES and one in particular *It Must Be Human*. But I think that it would be wrong not to leave well enough alone.[19]

All four tenants are developed within Stevens's verse. The first three examples are taken from prose presented to an academic audience in the early 1940s. The human question makes it weird; it appears in late 1954 in a letter to a critic in the last months of Stevens's life. Personally, I have been baffled by the qualifier "that it would be wrong *not* to leave well enough alone." Why the hesitation or ambiguity? What exactly is "it"? What exactly must be human?

Extraordinarily, Mack *must* make an ethical choice at the level of the scientific imagination: stuff it into the old mold, ignore it, or accept it as fact. Understood through supreme fiction, there is a choice: what *must it* be? What is abstracted in regression? Furthermore, the experiencer encounters such without decision, much like the obscure laws of a poet's spiritual crisis. When it is confronted, it stands outside possibility to both Mack and the experiencer. *It is incredible. I cannot ignore it. But is it more real than unreal?* If the *old mold* won't do, how to determine its credibility? What *must change* if not the mode of being in the world? The pleasure of it seems clearer, that despair has been thwarted and a new concept of humanity has been

---

18 Ibid., 679.
19 Stevens, *Letters of Wallace Stevens*, 863–64 (no. 955).

presented, hence: is it human? This runs directly into the alien self-concept, one which Mack and other researchers of the phenomenon have opined upon for decades. After all, when Mack received abductees, the distinction which defied psychiatric norms concerned "the fact they were discriminating individuals, largely of sound mind" and "inclined to doubt their experiences as was I."[20] Revealed were intrapersonal crises brought by obscure laws for which the experiencer and psychiatrist seek to reason. Mack and the abductees converge to rationalize what is normatively irrational. This is an affirmation of poetry itself. Such contributes to a properly moral and ethically situated revolution in scientific knowledge.[21]

After all, to receive experiencer testimony as had Mack is analogous to Stevens's poetic function. For one, the facilitator of a regression receives answers before questions or descriptions wholly irrational. Stevens, who analogously follows the incipience of the true subject, embarks on a similar experience. For Stevens and Mack regression analysis leads to a willful search for additional triggers — or more precise questions for the experiencer in general. For the poet, first let the poems be written and avoid the inimical. Trust retrospectively that they may be understood. Next assess the poetry of the subject and what it may disclose, if and only if one abides by the true subject by virtue of its fidelity to "the intelligence." What is disclosed is to be

---

20 Mack, *Abduction*, 10.

21 Recalling Kuhn's advice to Mack, some polarities of language dealt with in Stevens's theory of supreme fiction are, for example, real/unreal and objective/subjective. One term he uses for relation to the exterior of language is "region." Regions are sites of an absolute. At the point of mental abstraction (the immediate or that "it must be abstract"), notions of reality are carried by the imagination into human unreality. Such notions breach metaphysical consciousness. By virtue of a poet's sensibility, they are carried into human unreality (mediated consciousness, metabolically, thus "it must change"). In sum, metaphysical antinomies are resolved in regions exterior to any binarism of language, thus behind the stage and more into the stagecraft of anthropocentric consciousness. This absolute relation expands access to reality through the unreality of our existence in language (new concepts of reality are established thus "it must give pleasure").

accepted as insights into the nature of reality, or what was, up to the 1920s, more a natural mystery which by the 1930s had clear theoretical frameworks. In other words, when Mack encounters experiencers in the 1990s he was presented with a choice of fulfilment or despair. He chose affirmation, he chose fulfilment. This might be what Stevens means by "fictions which are extensions of reality,"[22] which involved the suspension of belief in an unreal world-fiction in order to access a superior reality. Such would be, from the vantage of base reality, unreal. Of course, this suggests a new reality when it may well be an expansion or parallel iteration.

---

22 Stevens, *Letters of Wallace Stevens,* 430 (no. 467).

8

Poetry Itself

A Few Baudelairean Monsters

When Charles Baudelaire published "Richard Wagner and Tannhäuser in Paris" (1861), he derided Parisians for their inability to grasp the composer's total work of art. He criticized critics for their pedantic emphases and inability to feel beyond what they had grown used to. Critics lacked a disposition that Wagner's *Gesamtkunstwerk* demanded, which led Baudelaire to delineate the character of the poet by two modes. The first is the instinctive poet; the second, a poet who becomes a critic superior to the critic itself. The former deserve pity if they never push past instinct, only to abide but not develop. Wagner was of the former, a strong poet who long since cultivated instinct into intellections, hence the *Gesamtkunstwerk* common critics failed to appraise. For Baudelaire, these critics were likely always such, having long since adopted a sophisticated lens to apprehend art which they seem incapable of changing; thus their view is *inimically* fixed, their character passive if not resembling the comforts of a religion. Baudelaire makes one caveat. The poet who overcomes their instinct inevitably becomes a superior critic. However, the critic who tries to become a poet results in a "monstrosity."[1]

If Baudelaire refers mainly to himself, his determinations track the passage of Wallace Stevens. However, we benefit from not drawing as hard of a line between modes of critic and poet. As we learned, Stevens's concept of abstraction emerges out of poetic instinct, which by the 1930s means to study intensively and develop a theory; to apply the abstraction of reality and determine such didactically, of which he had aversion. Baudelaire's description of the instinctive poet's rationale helps summarize Stevens's motive. For Baudelaire determined that poets who push through instinct are originally shaped by "a spiritual crisis [...] when they feel the need to reason about their art, to discover the obscure laws in virtue of which they have created, and extract from this study a set of precepts whose divine aim is infallibility in poetic creation."[2] This intrasubjective crisis concerns why and how a poet views and interacts in the world. This suggests an arcane source informs expressive compulsions, and is thus a crisis of spirit, mind, or *psyche*. At base something inexplicable happened, happens, or continues to happen which as crisis presents itself as an inevitable or unavoidable choice. A strong poet, as was Stevens, endeavors to develop an understanding of obscure laws through countermanding reality. The result is an innate power over conventional rationality and reason from within.[3] This, I find, summarizes both the production of his verse and the didactic task Stevens embarks upon in the 1930s.

If in the late modern era Baudelaire's superior critic is reprised through the figure of Stevens, his theoretical oeuvre is an exemplar of philosopher Hans Blumenberg's "secularization

---

[1] Charles Baudelaire, *The Painter of Modern Life and Other Essays,* trans. Johnathan Mayne (Phaidon Press, 2006), 124.

[2] Ibid.

[3] Harold Bloom's crisis concept supposes egoistic competition and historical pressure drive poetic creations. I always found it odd that Bloom premises his Stevens on a crisis he admittedly cannot prove. Harold Bloom, *Wallace Stevens: Poems of Our Climate* (Cornell University Press, 1976), 1–5.

thesis,"[4] which holds that scientific rationality did not evolve by eliminating or overcoming religious ideas but rather through reincorporating them. For Blumenberg, modernity uniquely redeploys perennial questions and answers lost through historical change. New knowledges are established, which often mean that "questions do not always precede their answers."[5] An immediate question is whether one should consider Stevens's thought religious. The same is true for aspects of ufology. If both are essentially questions of "why," many ufologists prefer to focus on the nuts and bolts of "how" craft work. Others take interest in the machinations of *arcana imperii* or the physiological effects of encounters with nonhuman beings. Stevens's concept of abstraction is also a matter of how, that is, how to transition from the irrational to the rational; from instinct to critique, toward a form of knowledge appropriately modern yet commensurable with "the intelligence" lost within the chaos of the nineteenth and twentieth centuries. In other words, Stevens's theory concerns what Blumenberg calls a misunderstanding of "credibility," where the acceptance of *answers before questions* is considered irrational by the status quo.[6] Blumenberg elevates such to "inconsistencies" that "appear in the system" yet lack "corresponding questions," hence face rejection by conventions of critical inquiry. Blumenberg concludes: "That this cannot be a purely rational operation is a lesson of history. If it is a lesson

---

4 "What mainly occurred in the process that is interpreted as secularization, at least (so far) in all but a few recognizable and specific instances, should be described not as the *transposition* of authentically theological contents into secularized alienation from their origin but rather as the reoccupation of answer positions that had become vacant and whose corresponding questions could not be eliminated." Hans Blumenberg, *The Legitimacy of the Modern Age,* trans. Robert M. Wallace (MIT Press, 1983), 65.

5 Ibid., 66.

6 Stevens's concept of disclosure does not mean the political dimensions of a later UFO disclosure, however, it is curiously situated as revealing to the poet what was otherwise sublated language within the poem he composes. Stevens presents his concept of credibility in distinction to normalizing the incredible in the prose "The Figure of the Youth as Virile Poet," in Wallace Stevens, *Collected Poetry and Prose* (Library of America, 1997), 666–85.

of anything."⁷ Therefore, if questions are sublated throughout the course of historical change, they will resurface when "new answers become due."⁸ These, in my estimation, concern the contemporary advance toward disclosure of the UFO phenomenon, which Stevens's theory is part of as an answer in wait.

Irrational Monsters: Nietzsche, Kierkegaard, and Coleridge

If a rationalist seeks to produce meaning, they need the irrational; just as the theist depends upon an atheist for meaning to be made of their own position. For how would a theist know what sets them forth if not considering or attempting by degree, the position of atheism? Insofar as the human condition is concerned, the twentieth century revealed that rationalism, when engorged and resolute, will become irrationalism. Thus, if rationalism requires an internal nemesis — the irrational — in order to police mysterious phenoms, it goes too far when it compromises humanity's survival. However, irrationalism is not the same as the irrational. The former is akin to absolute rationalism and the latter an appearance, quality, or view from within — a way out, one supposes.

While the irrational certainly persists throughout human history, modernity's irrationalists of the late eighteenth and nineteenth centuries is where we turn next. Following Blumenberg's thesis, Stevens inherits answers before questions from this period. Put another way, *poetry is the affirmation of the true subject*, and, as we have learned, questioning the poetry of the subject is *secondary yet essential* to self-disclosure. As part of the answer of disclosure, which is currently in the form of a question "are NHIs real?," Stevens's theory was equally backward to the official view of his time. A strong thinker, as was Stevens, inherently understood the irrational within a given paradigm. Successfully delivering it is yet another thing. This was Friedrich Nietzsche's instinctive principle albeit conveyed rationally (as long as he

---

7   Blumenberg, *The Legitimacy of the Modern Age*, 66.
8   Ibid.

were able). For over a century, his fate has fascinated us. It began with the Apollonian/Dionysian differentiation (order/chaos) and eventually arrives at "the will to power" or that which overcomes a primary binary in order to achieve a more profound, unheralded form of life. Following Nietzsche, Stevens similarly questioned whether supreme fiction must be human. Generally speaking, Nietzsche's path evolved into an irrational absolutism that Stevens avoids. Following Baudelaire, Nietzsche straddled the line between critic, poet, and monstrosity, whereas Stevens postulates monstrosity but ceases to pursue it.

Weirdly, to my mind, we associate Nietzsche most with philosophy, when he belonged first and foremost to language. By point of fact, he began as a philologist studying the language of historical texts. Because that is true, he approached the matter as a critic, a critical academic. However, through the ancient Greeks his transition to philosophy took form through an intense study of language. From there, he advanced upon the irrational in dramatic fashion against all other philosophy but his own. This was similarly the case for Søren Kierkegaard, yet no one I know associates these irrationalists with poetry. Are we mistaken not to? For poetry is language and then some. Put another way, what is an irrationalist philosopher if not parodic, absurd, or paradoxical? Kierkegaard did not want to be considered a philosopher, a fact consistently overlooked. If this were not precisely the case for Nietzsche, who thought himself a philosopher of the future, his insistence on radical subjectivity and disdain for Hegelianism sets him abreast. Therefore, if it were an intense experience with language that compelled them, should we not conclude philosophy was more a device than the heart of the matter? For philosophy takes place in language. Yet if it seems to take the place of language, what one finds is not philosophy but rather poetry itself. Therefore, what compelled their attacks on philosophy and to revolute existence as they had? What did they find through language which defied the perennial love of wisdom? For loving wisdom requires ethical and moral care; administering, not destroying philosophy.

To my mind, they are poet–critics who fought against philosophy's hegemonic legacy. The result would be love *sans sophia*. Like poets, their's an unwise love. Put another way, if the poet is the fool, the king is still upside down. Thus, a first point we shall return to: The basis of their view — theōria as philos "love" — was not irreducibly bound to sophia "theoretical wisdom."[9] The basis of philos was radically received, rejecting theoretical wisdom or judgment itself, for itself. Thus, a second point, the application of love as wisdom. Wisdom, it should be noted is *wise + doom;* wise + "inevitable danger, martyrdom, or terrible fate." When in the depths of the English language, Proto-Germanic reveals the truer sense of the word *wise:* "to see, to look, face."[10] And what does one face at the nether of inimical probing, if not the imagination at the exterior of language? Love is the outcome. Love, a view without judgment, the face of love within the imagination, is an infinite from reductions of self-illusion. Where else could one arrive if not to conclude the sovereignty of philosophy — this *doom of sophia* — was a fraudulent divinity administered by this or that poseur king? After all, *sophia* had long become phronesis or "practical wisdom" (and by extension formal then applied science), whereas love accords to a demiurgic refusal, a next step in human evolution.[11] In essence, are we slaves to man, or slaves to gods?

Poetry will involve itself in wisdom. When it does, we call it didactic poetry which uses artistic expression to teach, as it were, hence its practical and sophistic nature. This was useful for conveying messages and knowledge in ancient societies. But this is not the fundamental crux of "poetry itself." In the introduction to Stevens's collected prose and didactic poetry, *The Necessary Angel* (1951), he determines "poetry itself" to allow one to "disclose what he finds in his own poetry," thus the "disclosures of poetry" are "not disclosures of definitions of poetry" that is, not

---

9   F.E. Peters, *Greek Philosophical Terms: A Historical Lexicon* (New York University Press, 1967), 179.

10 Calvert Watkins, ed., *The American Heritage Dictionary of Indo-European Roots* (Houghton Mifflin Company, 1985), 74, s.v. "weid-."

11 Peters, *Greek Philosophical Terms*, 157.

sophia.¹² Poetry itself means "the naked poem, the imagination manifesting itself in its domination of words" and therefore concerns "a realization […] that is true" which "communicate to the reader the portent of the subject."¹³ Words are but imprints of the face of the imagination, a portent of the subject, that potent subject, which harkens back to "The Irrational Element in Poetry" (1936). It comes to this: "The real is constantly being engulfed in the unreal," thus poetry "is an illumination of a surface, the movement of a self in the rock," and a "force capable of bringing about fluctuations in reality in words free from mysticism," "a force independent of one's desire to elevate it."¹⁴

Poetry itself is not philosophy. It is not the love of wisdom; it concerns language and the intelligence that permeates from an exterior hence portent of the subject or potent subject. This is why Baudelaire determines that a poet must not remain passively instinctive yet warns of becoming a monstrosity (which I find particular to Nietzsche). This is also what Stevens determines as "advances […] to be made,"

> if the character of the poet was not so casual and intermittent a character. The poet cannot profess the irrational as the priest professes the unknown. The poet's role is broader, because he must be possessed, along with everything else, by the earth and by men in their earthy implications.¹⁵

Kierkegaard and Nietzsche arrive at a radical subjectivity and consequentially attempt to break philosophy from its claim on love. Through language they experience an exterior which is wholly irrational, say, an irrational element reifying the subjective truth as paramount within and without traditional rationalism. They find an undefined yet sufficient cause, what Stevens determines as "[s]omething of the unreal […] necessary to

---

12 Stevens, *Collected Poetry and Prose*, 639
13 Ibid.
14 Ibid., 639–40.
15 Ibid., 792.

fecundate the real; something of the sentimental [...] necessary to fecundate the anti-poetic."[16] By engorging the antipoetic, the *sophia* of philosophy, the effort means to break, if not reset, the technical destiny wisdom is condemned to.[17] Such enables a new understanding of *philos* to check a totalistic *sophia* or that sentimental tradition of rationalism governing the evolutionary energy of the soul as *psyche:* "breath of life, ghost, vital principle, anima."[18]

If Baudelaire's monsters mean to avoid irrationalism (as the absolutism of rationalism), we must add one who comes before them. For this was a similar conclusion had by Samuel Taylor Coleridge, who distinguishes between primary and secondary imagination as opposed to fancy. Primary imagination he defined as "the living Power and prime Agent of all human Perception, and as a repetition in the finite mind of the eternal act of creation in the infinite I AM."[19] As primary, the imagination is a single principle or source from *without*. It enters, shapes, or constitutes a local node or that repetitive, finite mind *within*. It is in existence by differentiation with the infinite, which the finite mind knows as "the infinite I AM" that is, in the end, irrational yet elemental.[20] Moreover, the "I AM" is a recognition of the potent subject to self. Secondary imagination is "an echo of" the primary,

> co-existing with the conscious will, yet still as identical with the primary in the kind of its operation. It dissolves, diffuses, dissipates, in order to recreate; or where this process is ren-

---

16 Ibid., 770.
17 "In effect, what we are remembering is the rather haggard background of the incredible, the imagination without intelligence, from which a younger figure is emerging, stepping forward in the company of a muse of its own, still half-beast and somehow more than human, a kind of sister of the Minotaur." Stevens, *Collected Poetry and Prose*, 675.
18 Peters, *Greek philosophical Terms*, 167.
19 I.A. Richards, *Coleridge on Imagination* (Indiana University Press, 1934), 57.
20 Elemental, i.e., quintessence, the fifth element or substance, aether, mind, and so forth.

dered impossible, yet still at all events it struggles to idealize and to unify. It is essentially vital, even as all objects (as objects) are essentially fixed and dead.[21]

By contrast, "fancy," as aptly summed by I.A. Richards, "collects and re-arranges, without re-making them, units of meaning already constituted by Imagination. In Imagination the mind is growing; in Fancy it is merely reassembling products of its past creation."[22]

Fancy is what Stevens refers to as "anti-poetic," whereas the "unreal" refers to "secondary imagination," which is an echo of the primary and the potent subject; of what it portends. Fancy is *sophia;* it has no direct access to the incessant imagination that vacates the inert world of objects established ahead of any administrator or caretaker. Crucial to this view is the openness of the secondary, that is, a return of an *unreal* to the *real* or "fecundation" of the primary. Secondary imagination is therefore open, as it has not yet achieved synthesis because "it struggles to idealize and unify." Therefore, it is a vital conscious substance as sufficient cause, viz. *psyche materialis.* Conversely, the fecundation of the anti-poetic is troubling, as it is already organized by the imagination ahead of "CHOICE" which restricts the efficacy of free will.[23] In no uncertain terms, this refers to the intelligence distinguished from an inimical free will of human intelligence. Why? The secondary returns to the primary ahead of any wise act, and so one is doomed to repeat, eternally, the same sequence albeit in what *should be* innumerable variations. And yet, are we not already far ahead with a similar calculation of all actual and possible transactions in our fanciful world through technologies of predication and convergence? Since the pandemic, have we not mistaken our world for an open world when in truth the open lies more and more within? Has not the mastery of space and relation forced the points of existence, local and facti-

---

21 Richards, *Coleridge on Imagination,* 58.
22 Ibid., 59.
23 Ibid., 57–59.

cal consciousnesses, inward to the without-always-ahead-of-us? Have we not transitioned from a Foucauldian heterotopia into a techno-hypertopia?

Stevens's unreal fecundates the real which regards an internal, intrapersonal relation. This relation informs *the intelligence* ahead of any fanciful schemata humans believe they administer. It is perhaps generative of a potent or infinite "I AM" that one consults. As the secondary echoes the primary, it remains open, defying a complete synthesis by fatal *sophia*. This is key to confronting incommensurability with the intelligence; it cannot remain an instinct and holds features of an actual free will. For Stevens, the "unreal" is simply the "credibility" of the imagination. Yet for the world of fancy it is pejoratively unreal, hence an irrational view. Fanciful *sophia* is obsessed not with "poetic fact" (the incommensurable open), but rather "absolute fact" or the closing sophistication. Fancy is the closure of the world from mind. Closure stops the processing between the irrational and the rational, which is contrarily the essence of science. What awaits if not a slave world of fewer and fewer kings, who want to rule over terms and conditions and impose a fanciful illusion? What do they achieve, if not a pathological *sophia* which "critiques the imagination"? Thus, the irrational element in poetry could be variations or dimensions of what is potentially fancy. It may be a secondary imagination informed by the primary. Accessing such requires not the inimical but rather abstraction for self-disclosure; abstraction from what remains of the open in the fanciful world of illusion, hence the poetry of the subject which follows the true subject. As to ufology, it may well be the basis for commensuration with interdimensional beings or those who operate with sciences and logics yet to be discovered or comprehended.

In sum, when Wallace Stevens remarks of abstraction "that everything has its origins in externals,"[24] he refers to the exterior of experienced language, the irrational element we cannot

---

24 Holly Stevens, ed., *Letters of Wallace Stevens* (University of California Press, 1966), 305 (no. 339).

define. Felt within, it determines the superiority of subjectivity, that it possess a truth greater than naturalist or materialist objectivity permits. What Stevens adds to knowledge is self-disclosure through abstraction, which affirms this subjective modality as rational—perhaps to reclaim a demiurgic mode. Abstraction, therefore, reveals that the irrational element in poetry concerns nonhuman intelligences as, or among, poetry itself. Thus, the distinction between *human intelligence* and *the intelligence* theorizes that which is not tradition. The truth remains irrational yet necessary to challenge our rationalistic slave world. The essence of this can be found in "The Irrational Element in Poetry":

> What interests us is a particular process in the rational mind which we recognize as irrational in the sense that it takes place unaccountably. Or, rather, I should say that what interests us is not so much the Hegelian process as what comes of it. We should probably be much more intelligently interested if from the history of the irrational there had developed a tradition. [... T]he only reason why it does not yet have a tradition is that its tradition is in progress.[25]

If we return to the mutual dependence between irrationalist and rationalist, the exchange between points of difference would always be in progress. But that is a simplification that risks relative stances and indeterminate conclusions. While such may be predominant modes, there are synthetic moments wherefrom new knowledges are traced out, albeit fragile and fleeting. This has remained the case for Stevens's theory and specific occasions of his verse that take the posture of the would-be demiurge. And it is my conceit that this synthesis is upon us with the UFO phe-

---

25 Stevens, *Collected Poetry and Prose*, 782–83. The above is characteristic of "the disclosures of poetry" which concern "the disclosure of the individuality of the poet." Such knowing is hinged upon a historical concept uncannily similar to Blumenberg's thesis. See ibid., 783–84.

nomenon. We will not yet become gods. Ours is either an era of the demiurge or the slave.

Poetry and Philosophy

As with Coleridge, Baudelaire, Kierkegaard, Nietzsche, and Stevens, theory is primarily *philos* or the core of what the pre-Socratics termed *theōria*. *Theōria* informs the basis of what I call an ethics of the imagination or poetry's eventual *sophia*. Fundamentally it concerns two things. First, a validation of our ability to view with the mind, to dream beyond the closed concept of human existence and its antagonism with essentialism. Second, the practical application of this view; to develop and deploy an apparatus of imaginative capture — what situates reflective thought with *the intelligence*. It is precisely this situating that Stevens considers "disclosure [...] certainly to myself."[26] Such is hypothesized as the basis of human knowing; what Stevens's late prose suggests as proto-epistemic or "a poetry of thought."[27]

Historically, *theōria* belonged more to poetry and less to what we today call philosophy. Thus, as the predecessor to modern science, philosophy sought to measure what is and is not "actual" or "there," placing emphasis on formulating questions of measurement and process. Over time, philosophical metaphysics appropriated the living efficacy of the dream and renamed it "being." Until the advent of psychology this effectively displaced dreaming from scientific legitimacy. Philosophy's science of being — metaphysics — evolved into distinct methodologies such as theology, logic, and mathematics. Through the late Romantic and Idealist periods particular to the West, philosophy continued to assume the point of its own genesis — poetry itself — as its own. By consequence, poetry became more and more a pejorative enduring the fate of *sophia*. However, philosophy failed to completely consolidate poetry into a concept, which thus remained a form of a greater formlessness — that source of

---

26 Ibid., 784.
27 Ibid., 854.

revolutionary anomalies that Thomas Kuhn determines within "normal science."[28] As the single global narrative that philosophy wanted to impose continued to fail, materialist, positivist, and naturalist modes of science, as well as formal, applied, and practical variations, flourished. Pure theory waned and patternicity ascended through technoscientific thought, namely by the work of Bruno Latour and others. If what we broadly categorize as NHI suggests to unify *philos* + *sophia* once again, it is crucial to understand the collapse of philosophical legitimacy, and what it has since struggled to overcome, as intimated by the likes of Nietzsche, Kierkegaard, and Coleridge — to which I add Stevens (to be sure there are many others). Such crisis was contemplated at length by the philosopher Georg W.F. Hegel (1770-1831) who, by the nineteenth century described such by way of an owl:

> [P]hilosophy, as the thought of the world, does not appear until reality has completed its formative process, and made itself ready. History thus corroborates the teaching of the conception that only in the maturity of reality does the ideal appear as counterpart to the real, apprehends the real world in its substance, and shapes it into an intellectual kingdom. When philosophy paints its grey in grey, one form of life has become old, and by means of grey it cannot be rejuvenated, but only known. The owl of Minerva takes its flight only when the shades of night are gathering.[29]

The formative process of reality is derived from what, if not the irrational. Hence the "thought of the world" is not ready until the irrational is fully conceived. From the perspective of Stevens, as well as Hans Blumenberg, overcoming the irrational is problematic and hence provides pure theory as our predomi-

---

28 Thomas Kuhn's well-known distinction between normal and anomalous science tracks neatly with what Stevens nearly two decades prior called the imagination as "irrepressible revolutionist." Thomas Kuhn, *The Structure of Scientific Revolutions,* 2nd ed. (University of Chicago Press, 1970), 5.

29 Georg W.F. Hegel, *The Philosophy of Right,* trans. S.W. Dyde (Batoche Books, 2001), 20.

nant prior. Do the words of Hegel mean the maturity of reality is underway in terms of our perceptive capacity and bodily limitations? After all, we rely on technologies to make the irrational legible thus made-meld into our contemporary "thought of the world." Precisely what is the thought of the world, if not artificial intelligence and technoscience, the lurch of *sophia*? Is this thought not thinking without the Heideggerian open? What is it like, a mere thought already perceived by a subject in an instant, without relational space, only to vanish?[30]

For Hegel, *history* is an antagonist that presents a "corroborative" testimony. It teaches that the ideal and real are counterparts headed to final synthesis. These counterparts apprehend — literally arrest — the world and deny a vital, primary substance establishing a global facsimile in its place. From this, an intellectual kingdom cleaves its world from nature. What is the substance of this world then, if not given nature or the mind? As this would mean to freeze all movement, dynamic, life, if not everything, into total inertness or, perhaps, a stupidly automated fancy, some kingdom of Bostromic paperclips. What does it replay, if not geocentric ignorance at a different scale? Thus, one form of life, humanity, is old and cannot be resuscitated, simply known, hence the owl takes flight. But that it takes flight is critical; the transition is incomplete.

Hegel's end of the world is apocalyptical before freed by totality, the doom of *sophia*, a loveless, dead world. Thus it should not surprise us to recall that the statue in Stevens's "Owl's Clover" takes flight "to space. To space?"[31] Are we to become the owl? Is the owl what "shapes" the character of the poet who inherently

---

30 Throughout the *Basic Writings*, commentaries define Martin Heidegger's "the open" and "openness" in varying ways. Generally, the revealing of being(s) is a matter of accidents which show us the world by virtue of revealing. Thus "being-in-the-world" concerns Heidegger's Dasein or space where beings reveal themselves "out of concealment" and "into their 'truth' (*alētheia*)" only to withdraw "again into obscurity." David Farrell Krell, "General Introduction: The Question of Being," in Martin Heidegger, *Basic Writings*, ed. David Farrell Krell (Harper San Fransisco, 1993), 20.

31 Stevens, *Collected Poetry and Prose*, 169.

understands "constant shaping, as distinguished from constancy of shape?"[32] What Stevens describes in the late 1940s resounds the formless truth governing history; that poetry's form is an anomalous refusal of final concepts because it is irrational yet elemental, energetic, psychical, soulful, a love without judgment that moves laterally through dimensions *ad infinitum*. To that Stevens asked if truth shapes the unreality always upon us. If so, would not belief triumph over a constant shape that requires a consistent identity over infinite resemblance? Resemblance is paramount and proliferate in that Coleridgean secondary, for Stevens was not interested in "philosophic poetry," which had "done so much to strengthen the critics of poetry in their attacks on the poetry of thought"[33] and this, I need to add, profanes Hegel's dead "thought of the world" in other words, fancy.

Once more, didactic poetry is not poetry itself. For Hegel overemphasizes the idea and collapses into the inimical paranoia of the mad sovereign. A total rationality kills everything by a royal rational irrationalism. If Stevens eschews such in "A Collect of Philosophy" (1951), it is likely he had the above passage of Hegel in mind:

> Theoretically, the poetry of thought should be the supreme poetry. Hegel called poetry the art of arts, specifically because in poetry the material of which the poem is made, that is to say, the language of the poem, is wholly subordinated to the idea.[34]

Language as the material of the poem says nothing of mind or of an exterior to language itself. While this is a problematic passage (material/idea) here, we are best to contrast a "poetry of thought" with Hegel's "thought of the world." In sum, the poetry of thought comes after the arresting of irrational substance

---

32 Ibid., 818.
33 Ibid., 854.
34 Ibid.

(or the apocalyptic assumption, supposing we escape sophia). Hence Stevens, continuing, remarks:

> It is very easy to imagine a poetry of ideas in which the particulars of reality would be shadows among the poem's disclosures. If we are to dismiss from poetry expectations of that nature, we might equally well dismiss from philosophy all the profound expectations on which it is based.[35]

Stevens remarks on philosophy's legitimacy crisis: A crisis which supposes poetry itself as Hegel's "intellectual kingdom" or mastery of "the real world in its substance." For the poet, *mind beyond being* is the real, a metalogic in language contrary to the doom of *sophia*. Conversely, the poem of poems brings about disclosures that coat this kingdom under shadows of the owl's wings, hence *particulars of reality*. Then history is merely corroborative, a dynamic mechanism which enmeshes a shaper but does not fully apprehend it. Reality is ever open to the shaper, viz. poetic mechanism, which serves as an ethical matter of an apparent free will. Here the triumph of the imagination, following Stevens, is a carrier of an infinite if not redemptive real. Considerations of what *sophia* attempts to subsume appear in "Imagination as Value" (1948). Stevens defines it this way:

> The truth seems to be that we live in concepts of the imagination before the reason has established them. If this is true, then reason is simply the methodizer of the imagination. It may be that the imagination is a miracle of logic and that its exquisite divinations are calculations beyond analysis, as the conclusions of the reason are calculations wholly within analysis.[36]

---

35 Ibid. And: "A poem in which the poet has chosen for his subject a philosophic theme should result in the poem of poems. That the wing of poetry should also be the rushing wing of meaning seems to be an extreme aesthetic good; and so in time and perhaps, in other politics, it may come to be." Ibid.

36 Ibid., 738.

"Analysis" means the limits of formal or applied technosciences which depend upon classic logic. "Calculations beyond" clearly refer to metalogic outside of it; once more, poetry itself. In other words, Stevens's check on the hubris of philosophy moves beyond Hegel's "grey in grey" or chiaroscuro as static syntheses: theist/atheist, rationalist/irrationalist. How else to interpret the owl of Minerva, whose flight ensues "only when the shades of night are gathering," which for Stevens are "shadows among the poem's disclosure" — of reality, a glimpse of the open. Hence, "chiaroscuro," which appears a handful of times in Stevens's oeuvre, is reminiscent of "voluble shadows."[37] Thus when grey is grey, come shadows wherefrom reality discloses through the imagination — the owl evades capture. This thinking was operative as early as "The Irrational Element in Poetry":

> Just so, there are those who, having never yet been convinced that the rational has quite made us divine, are willing to assume the efficacy of the irrational in that respect. The rational mind, dealing with the known, expects to find it glistening in a familiar ether. What it really finds is the unknown always behind and beyond the known, giving it the appearance, at best, of chiaroscuro.[38]

Philosophy's crisis was documented a century after Hegel by one of the most famous philosophers of late modernity, Martin Heidegger, who in the 1930s confronted the "oblivion of being" and made a "turn to poetry" doubling down on language.[39] Knowing Hegel struggled to synthesize poetry into a category of philosophy, Heidegger acknowledged philosophy's progenic crisis for the modern ear and subsequently birthed the

---

37 Stevens, *Letters of Wallace Stevens*, 62 (no. 67).

38 Stevens, *Collected Poetry and Prose*, 791.

39 "This turning is not a change of standpoint from Being and Time, but in it the thinking that was sought first arrives at the location of that dimension out of which Being and Time is experienced, that is to say, experienced from the fundamental experience of the oblivion of Being." Martin Heidegger, "Letter on Humanism," in *Basic Writings,* 231–32.

postmodern mouth. By the 1950s, Heidegger's writing became increasingly enigmatic, for example "The Question Concerning Technology."[40] When criticizing those who sought to *elevate philosophy to a science,* Heidegger acknowledged that poetry concerns an exterior to the foundations of human knowledge.[41] If his obsession with poetry's fundamental "essence"[42] was akin to philosophical heroism, it concerns a drama paradoxically hinged upon dreaming and being; a link philosophy originally obscures then, in despair, desperately seeks.

That philosophy's crises coincide with exponential leaps in computational capacity and technological proliferation is not coincidental — rather that the thought of the world approaches, that the pure theory associated with "thinking" is necrotic. Yet through Heidegger's example, poetry responds to the epistemological crisis brought about by what he terms *Technik.* If at first this means that philosophical being relinquishes an ancient task as the jailor of dreaming (perhaps that agonistic "mis-prision" to which Harold Bloom once referred), it does not preclude a new jailor replacing it.[43] Critical to the technoscientific moment are the *means* of poetry to develop new knowledge under the reins of *Technik.* In other words, if Heidegger discovers *philos,* poetry itself could save *sophia,* wisdom, "fate, doom, martyrdom." It ultimately concerns an immeasurable form that he tries to affirm, one that Stevens propounds as "even older than the ancient world."[44] Thus Stevens's "supreme fiction" and speculation of human artificiality concerns *theōria* as the view, and then practice or application of this form: love without judgment of the nonhumans among us which may well be us. The imagi-

---

40 Martin Heidegger, "The Question Concerning Technology," in *Basic Writings,* 307–42.
41 Analogously, what Charles Taylor deemed the "overcoming of epistemology." Charles Taylor, "Overcoming Epistemology," in *Philosophical Arguments* (Harvard University Press, 1995), 12.
42 See Heidegger, *Basic Writings,* 202, 260, 339.
43 Harold Bloom, *The Anxiety of Influence: A Theory of Poetry* (Oxford University Press, 1973), xvii.
44 Stevens, *Collected Poetry and Prose,* 732.

nation is integral to our evolutionary continuity. This concerns contemporary scientific knowledge that, as with any content of consciousness, *is subject to change,* which means *subject to the form of poetry itself;* an understanding of reality otherwise pejoratively shunned as panpsychist heresy. It comes to this: following Gaston Bachelard, individuals are tasked to overcome epistemological obstacles, thus rupture *sophia,* by way of an unconscious incipience; barriers to the progress of scientific knowledge and not the establishment of scientific authoritarianism. Rupture is the breaking point in normal science, hence the spout of an incommensurable poetics, a true phenomenon in wait for conceptualization thus generative of yet another. Following Thomas Kuhn, "normal science" hosts "revolutionary science" as perturbant anomalies within epistemic or scientific knowledge. This is the essential situation of Stevens's theory of poetry and self-disclosure.

Stevens's Monstrosity

Before the 1930s, Stevens's heroism did not concern *sophia,* but rather *philos.* However, when Stevens approached academia in the 1940s, his coming to terms with the phenomenon led to didactic criticism directed at attending philosophers. This came in the form of his "intimidating thesis" as found in "The Figure of the Youth as Virile Poet" (1943):

> [T]here are so many things which, as they are, and without any intervention of the imagination, seem to be imaginative objects that it is no doubt true that absolute fact includes everything that the imagination includes.[45]

This suggests that "the imagination" exceeds the human will to imagine — which implies more than simple self-deception. Absolute fact denies the irrational element from within one's mental view apropos to Coleridge and Baudelaire. Therefore, if

---
45 Ibid., 681.

it's "absolute fact" we need "rescue" from, it arrives as didactic heroism. Apologetically, Stevens means to check self-deception which obscures "poetic truth" by cutting relation to a real. Thus if "The Figure of the Youth as Virile Poet" states that for philosophers "facts" are "possibly beyond their perception in the first instance and outside the normal range of their sensibility,"[46] Stevens's heroic *philos* responds to the ancient displacement of poetry by philosophy. This was evident by 1943 as he reprises concepts of sensibility originally formulated in "The Irrational Element in Poetry" (1936). Then he was more tepid: "I am not competent to discuss reality as a philosopher."[47] Yet by 1943 he insists on the limits of "philosophic truth," declaring the most hardened eventually "turn to poetic truth," thus "return to their starting-point" having first come to "despair."[48] By way of Nietzsche his insistence on absolute fact results in his own parodic absurdity. This would be Stevens's intimidating thesis and the peak of his own monstrosity.

Nonetheless, if his concern was a relation with a real, he refines this thesis in "Three Academic Pieces" (1947). There, identity and resemblance concern passages within a metaphoric field. This concerns "praeternature," speculated to exceed materialism and naturalism. Things, in his conception, are resemblances or facets projected by an absolute object.[49] Thus, within the metaphoric field — secondary *theōria* as a view — the completed object escapes the "derogatory" which is "a truth about poetry."[50] This is "one of the principles that compose the theory of poetry," "that poetry is part of the structure of reality."[51] What keeps "truth" from a mental view is desire for absolute fact, the default mode seeking an identity itself.[52]

---

46 Ibid., 680.
47 Ibid., 781.
48 Ibid., 680.
49 Ibid., 687.
50 Ibid., 692.
51 Ibid.
52 Stevens's "The Noble Rider and the Sound of Words" insists that this practice extends to all objects we encounter. If so, it means that poems are

What changed Stevens's attitude? What's behind his insistence of a "starting-point?" I suspect his despair was partially overcome and that the *starting point* concerns innumerable phases of metaphysics linked to interventions of an "irrepressible revolutionist,"[53] an imagination irrespective of human will. A strong indication of despair was noted at the end of 1942s "Landscape with Boat": recall "he might be truth, himself, or part of it."[54] Despair may be why Stevens, in "The Figure of the Youth as Virile Poet," implores attendees of his lecture, some who were philosophers, to abandon obsessions with absolute fact. He more or less insults those with limited "perception" and claims they are not "outside the normal range of [...] sensibility."[55] For some, this would prove the poet's pomposity or aloofness. Such accusations do not answer why he made such comments. We have to consider what "truth" means, rather that he was "part of it."[56]

Perhaps Stevens's insults are better understood as a growing awareness of NHI. Chronologically, "Owl's Clover" (1935) reprises experiences we classify today with the UFO phenomenon. "The Irrational Element in Poetry," a lecture delivered in late 1936, theorizes this encounter as "poetic truth" or transpo-

---

    special objects, as they provide access to special elements of consciousness; they retain by access to "regions." Stevens, as with other strong poets, believes that the poem guards the passage between reflective thought and the intelligence. For example, in "Three Academic Pieces" Stevens presents concepts of an absolute object. Such concerns "an imitation of something in nature" which "may even surpass identity and assume a praeternature," thus a notional incipience "may escape the derogatory." Here he suggests identifying something phenomenal or anomalous "is the vanishing-point of resemblance." Resemblance is therefore superior to identity in that the former concerns fixity and conceals an anomaly's truer nature. Resemblance confronts an inadequate stance of naturalistic self-deception: "Nature is not mechanical [...]. Its prodigy is not identity but resemblance and its universe of reproduction is not an assembly line but an incessant creation." Ibid., 687.

53 Ibid., 736.
54 Ibid., 220.
55 Ibid., 680.
56 Ibid., 220.

sitions between subjective experience and objective reality.[57] The subject/object distinction, as we have seen, is dissolved in poetry yet generative of a praeternatural beyond which permits the structuring of reality.[58] For instance, he finds himself in the statue. In other places, he is in a rock. While it is easy to dismiss poetry as panpsychic nonsense, I consider this a base function of poetic self-disclosure, as that which concerns commensurability with NHI. Thus, by the early 1940s Stevens reprises the matter as transitions from the "incredible" to the "credible," noting that in the establishment of "general progress [...] poetry has participated"[59] — fitting him squarely with Blumenberg's later secularization thesis. And so, by the late 1940s the poems and prose attempt to consolidate the matter, seeking validation as theory to a broader academic audience, which is why Stevens is eventually more conciliatory to philosophy if only wanting to institute, as a proper monster, a new *sophia*.

Returning to the early 1940s, we find a notion of "general progress" which informs the original polemic against logical positivism, a counter-critical move against the "official view of being."[60] This suggests that there are other beings who know better. That is, Stevens's victimization turns dramatic when he defines the poet's life as "apart from politics [...] lived [...] in a radiant and productive atmosphere."[61] He presents himself a poet living a life that "is the life of that atmosphere" and "there the philosopher is an alien."[62] Such life is based on a "pleasure of agreement with the radiant and productive world in which he lives,"[63] whereas the philosopher owns despair in his endless bemoaning, locked within the artifice of an inferior free will.

---

57 Ibid., 676.
58 I suspect Stevens adopts this from Richards's *Coleridge on Imagination*, specifically the chapter "The Coalescence of Subject and Object," 44–71.
59 Stevens, *Collected Poetry and Prose*, 679.
60 Ibid., 667.
61 Ibid., 678.
62 Ibid.
63 Ibid.

What to make of the philosopher as alien? It as if Stevens speaks from the vantage of NHI. Let's consider the late poem "A Discovery of Thought":

> The first word would be of the susceptible being arrived,
> The immaculate disclosure of the secret, no more obscured.
> The sprawling of winter might suddenly stand erect,
>
> Pronouncing its new life and ours, not autumn's prodigal returned,
> But an antipodal, far-fetched creature, worthy of birth,
> The true tone of the metal of winter in what it says:
>
> The accent of deviation in the living thing
> That is its life preserved, the effort to be born
> Surviving being born, the event of life.[64]

The "first word" Stevens references claims dreaming as a productive element from reality. Says Stevens:

> It is the *mundo* of the imagination in which the imaginative man delights and not the gaunt world of the reason. The pleasure is the pleasure of powers that create a truth that cannot be arrived at by the reason alone, a truth that the poet recognizes by sensation. The morality of the poet's radiant and productive atmosphere is the morality of the right sensation.[65]

By 1934, it concerns an unreal of secondary imagination which fecundates by a real of primary imagination. The concern were a fecundation of the antipoetic or closing of the world into *sophia*. At this time, Stevens had only begun his theory of poetry and was in the midst of a developing his concept of abstraction. Recall that in 1936 the innumerable *starting point* concerns "the

---

64 Ibid., 459.
65 Ibid., 679.

THE POET AS EXPERIENCER

transposition of an objective reality to a subjective reality"[66] as found in "The Irrational Element in Poetry," which propounds the key concepts of poetic function and disclosure of the intelligence as poetic mechanism. By 1943 it is recoded to mean transitions from the incredible to the credible:

> The incredible is not a part of poetic truth. On the contrary, what concerns us in poetry, as in everything else, is the belief of credible people in credible things. It follows that poetic truth is the truth of credible things, not so much that it is actually so as that it must be so. It is toward that alone that it is possible for the intelligence to move.[67]

If the 1930s are incredible, so says "Owl's Clover," there's a truth problem which "The Irrational Element in Poetry" didacticizes. This intrasubjective crisis feeds his impetuosity for years to come. Thus, by 1943, all facts are supposed by poetic truth, and this truth he is part of. By 1947, this concerns a relation or ongoing dialogical situation regarding what 1942s "A Discovery of Thought" implies: ongoing NHI encounters. Stevens's theory is an effort which fails to convince the academic status quo. In a way, one could pity Stevens and, at the same time, admire his resilience. Yet we are foolish to think that despair was his primary concern, and equally to think he never experienced such.

Stevens's "intimidating thesis" concerns more than naïve metaphysics. After all, he conceived of the imagination as a way to "triumph over the incredible,"[68] and NHI may be how he comes to this truth. Writes Stevens:

> What we have called elevation and elation on the part of the poet, which he communicates to the reader, may be not so much elevation as an incandescence of the intelligence and so more than ever a triumph over the incredible. Here as part

---

66 Ibid., 781.
67 Ibid., 675.
68 Ibid., 680.

of the purification that all of us undergo as we approach any central purity, and that we feel in its presence.[69]

That we "feel in its presence" tempts a false positive. However, it is an "it" and otherwise unidentified. What to make of "purification" and "central purity?" Let us reconsider Stevens's concept of reality in terms of fact, for this concerned "genuine poetic activity" which regards "the general progress from the incredible to the credible," "a progress in which poetry has participated."[70] There he notes an ethics or "the integrity and peculiarity of the poetic character" that "the poet must get rid of the hieratic in everything that concerns him and must move constantly in the direction of the credible."[71] Indeed, this feints secularism if only to exceed it. The poet does this because he subsequently "must create his unreal out of what is real."[72]

A poet's unreal commutates with the intelligence of a real and will continue to disclose by the intelligence. But it is not an elevation, but rather a returning to a reality which resembles, yet not identifying the ultimate prior. Thus, reality has expanded by the "unreal" that Stevens refers to, or the starting point of a naïve metaphysics which is originally illiberal to the prior and hidden reality as unreality, thus with regard to possibilities of knowledge expansion. When he regards an "agreement with reality," it means to dissolve metaphysical excess within our own ideation. By its disappearance, metaphysical experience expands reality through poetic truth. Reality, which had been irrelevant for the naïve, grants an intrasubjective validation. This concerns *credibility* hinged upon "the nature of our experience" and for this he quotes William James.[73] Stevens's position is that *poetry* and *poetic creations* have contributed to a "general" progression of reality through phases of metaphysical experience that human knowledge must develop to evolve further. Failure to under-

---

69 Ibid.
70 Ibid., 679.
71 Ibid.
72 Ibid.
73 Ibid.

stand phases of metaphysics makes the progression of knowledge rigid and fixed — which denies the notion of any "praeternature."[74]

The poetry of thought — the unreality made from commutation with a real — is proto-epistemic until such notions are disclosed. They arrive in poetry and the arts, as they do in sciences. Central to Stevens's polemic are successive phases of intrasubjectification lost on the official view, yet generative of new knowing. For the officium is concerned not with epistemological progression, but rather with a perverse conservatism that fears historical metaphysics (secondary imagination), hence its suppression by an analytical *sophia*. If the lover of absolute fact confuses poetic truth with a naïve pejorative, it is due to an ahistoric *irrepressibility* that Stevens experiences as a poet. Here the imagination is a revolutionist in a nonvolitious way, as it attempts, in an egoistic frame waxing victim, to disclose unwittingly from the intelligence. In other words, I suppose Stevens as experiencer makes it possible to reject the predecessor — naïve metaphysics — by the progenic form that displaced it: a naïve realism of the 1930s. And here Stevens may be aligned with metaphysical realism — "Aristotelians are not brutes"[75] — that metaphysics itself or secondary imagination (a proper regard for our unreality) is what we lack in our obsession with absolute fact.

Stevens's self-referencing concerns his growth as a poet. He speaks as an experiencer of poetry itself. A disavowal of metaphysics denies a deeper element of reality from comprehension. Strong poets begin with naïve metaphysics. Conversely, when one self-deceives one denies future detection of a nonanthropomorphic agent. The failure to affirm metaphysics is more than *hierophantic* or hiero-fancy, it means that we deny psychical growth of a real. However, where *poetic creation* concerns credibility, the fact that the arrival at either/or, realist, or metaphysician is an error prone for despair. The metaphysician becomes a

---

74 Ibid., 687.
75 Ibid., 783.

charlatan and, in their persistence, the realist suffers from absolute illusions.

Bibliography

7NEWS Australia. "David Grusch UFO/UAP bombshells: Ross Coulthart reveals the inside story." *YouTube,* July 27, 2023. https://www.youtube.com/watch?v=x_9gTDXF9Vc.

Alighieri, Dante. *The New Life.* Translated by J.G. Nichols. Herperus, 2003.

Angelucci, Orfeo M. *The Secret of the Saucers.* Amherst Press, 1955.

Baudelaire, Charles. *The Painter of Modern Life and Other Essays.* Translated by Johnathan Mayne. Phaidon Press, 2006.

Bloom, Harold. *Wallace Stevens: Poems of Our Climate.* Cornell University Press, 1976.

Benjamin, Walter. "On Some Motifs in Baudelaire." In *Walter Benjmain Selected Writings,* Vol. 4: *1938–1940: Fruits of Exile,* edited by Howard Eiland and Michael W. Jennings, translated by Edmund Jephcott. The Belknap Press of Harvard University Press, 2003.

Blumenberg, Hans. *The Legitimacy of the Modern Age.* Translated by Robert M. Wallace. MIT Press, 1983.

BookwormHistory. "The Ramble Cave." *Atlas Obscura,* October 2, 2015. https://www.atlasobscura.com/places/the-ramble-cave-new-york-new-york.

Brazaeu, Peter. *Parts of a World: Wallace Stevens Remembered.* Random House, 1983.

Burt, Eugene H. *UFOs and Diamagnetism: Correlations of UFO and Scientific Observations.* Exposition Press, 1970.

Coe, Albert. *The Shocking Truth.* 1969.

Cook, Elanor. *Reader's Guide to Wallace Stevens.* Princeton University Press, 2007.

Cooper, Helene, Ralph Blumenthal, and Leslie Kean. "Glowing Auras and 'Black Money': The Pentagon's Mysterious U.F.O. Program." *The New York Times,* December 16, 2017. https://www.nytimes.com/2017/12/16/us/politics/pentagon-program-ufo-harry-reid.html.

Clelland, Mike. *The Messengers: Owls, Synchronicity and the UFO Abductee.* Beneath the Stars Press, 2020.

Dolan, Richard M. *UFOs for the 21st Century Mind: The Definitive Guide to the UFO Mystery.* New and Expanded Edition. Richard Dolan Press, 2023.

Eyes on Cinema. "Abductees and Researchers Talk About the Alien Abduction Phenomenon, April 1993." *YouTube,* September 2, 2022. https://www.youtube.com/watch?v=Gw4o-Qd4jlA.

Global News. "UFO hearing: Eyewitnesses describe encounters with 'non human' entities to Congress | FULL." *YouTube,* July 26, 2023. https://www.youtube.com/watch?v=OwSkXDmV6Io.

Greer, Steven M. *Hidden Truth: Forbidden Knowledge.* ZTT Consulting, 2013.

Groves, Adam Staley. "The Poetic Subject: A Theory of Poetry According to the Poet Wallace Stevens and the Philosopher Jean Wahl." PhD diss., University of Aberdeen, 2016.

Hegel, Georg W.F. *The Philosophy of Right.* Translated by S.W. Dyde. Batoche Books, 2001.

Heidegger, Martin. *Basic Writings.* Edited by David Farrell Krell. Harper, 1993.

Hopkins, Budd. *Missing Time: A Documented Study of UFO Abductions.* Richard Marek Publishers, 1981.

Jones, Danny. "NASA's Forbidden Alien Study Finds Proof of Spiritual Beings | Chris & Emily Bledsoe." *YouTube,* December 4, 2023. https://www.youtube.com/watch?v=XmVQFX2Pp60.

Jung, C.G. *Flying Saucers: A Modern Myth of Things Seen in the Sky.* Translated by R.F.C. Hull. Princeton University Press, 1978.

———. "Parcelsus the Physician I." In *The Collected Works of C.G. Jung,* Vol. 15: *Spirit in Man, Art, and Literature,* edited and translated by Gerhard Adler, edited by Herbert Read, Michael Fordham, and William McGuire. Princeton University Press, 1983.

Lacatski, James, Colm Kelleher, and George Knapp. *Inside the US Government Covert UFO Program: Initial Revelations.* RTMA, 2023.

Mack, John E. *Abduction: Human Encounters with Aliens.* Scribner, 1994.

———. *Passport to the Cosmos.* White Crow Books, 1999.

Masters, Michael. *The Extratempestral Model.* Full Circle Press, 2022.

Pasulka, D.W. *American Cosmic: UFOs, Religion, Technology.* Oxford University Press, 2019.

Peters, F.E. *Greek Philosophical Terms: A Historical Lexicon.* New York University Press, 1967.

Richards, I.A. *Coleridge on Imagination.* Indiana University Press, 1934.

"Rockland U.F.O. 'Invasion' Starts Round of Explanations." *The New York Times,* October 11, 1976. https://www.nytimes.com/1976/10/11/archives/rockland-ufo-invasion-starts-round-of-explanations.html.

Rock Products News. "Former New York Quarry May Get New Life." *Rock Products,* March 28, 2019. https://rockproducts.com/2019/03/28/former-new-york-quarry-may-get-new-life/.

SALT, "'Zero Doubt' Non-Human Intelligence on Earth – Col. Karl Nell & Alex Klokus | SALT iConnections NY."

YouTube, May 22, 2024. https://www.youtube.com/watch?v=RploFrdJWfs.

Saving VHS Tapes. "The Hudson Valley UFO Sightings Dr. J. Allen Hynek, Phillip J. Imbrogo – Close Encounters of the 4th Kind." *YouTube,* November, 27, 2020. https://www.youtube.com/watch?v=2fQgrYLUfjo.

Serio, John, ed. *The Cambridge Companion to Wallace Stevens.* Cambridge University Press, 2007.

Stevens, Holly, ed. *Letters of Wallace Stevens.* University of California Press, 1966.

Stevens, Wallace. *Collected Poetry and Prose. The Library of America,* 1997.

Taylor, Charles. "Overcoming Epistemology." In *Philosophical Arguments.* Harvard University Press, 1995.

To The Stars: Bringing You the Future. https://tothestars.media/pages/about.

Vallee, Jacques. *Alien Contact Trilogy,* Vol. 1: *Dimensions: A Casebook of Alien Contact.* Anomalist Books, 2003).

———. *Passport to Magonia: From Folklore to Flying Saucers.* Daily Grail Publishing, 1969.

Wahl, Jean. *The Philosopher's Way.* Oxford University Press, 1948.

Watkins, Calvert, ed. *The American Heritage Dictionary of Indo-European Roots.* Houghton Mifflin Company, 1985.